JOY IN THE JOURNEY

Guy Rice Doud

JOY IN THE JOURNEY

Guy Rice Doud

PUBLISHING

COLORADO SPRINGS, COLORADO

Library of Congress Cataloging–in–Publication Data

Doud, Guy Rice, 1953-

    When you surrender your self-sufficiency and lean on Christ, you
discover — Joy in the Journey / by Guy Rice Doud

    p. cm.

    ISBN 1-56179-092-3

    1. Doud, Guy Rice, 1953 . 2. Christian biography — Minnesota. 3. High
school teachers — Minnesota — Biography. I. Title. II. Title: Joy in the
Journey.
BF1725.D68A3 1992
248.4—dc20

                          92-18947
                             CIP

Published by Focus on the Family Publishing, Colorado Springs, CO 80995

Unless otherwise noted, Scripture quotations are from The Holy Bible, New
International Version, copyright 1973, 1978, 1984 by the International Bible Society.

Permissions

"Friends" written by Michael W. Smith and Deborah D. Smith. © Copyright 1982, Meadowgreen Music
Co., 2505 21st Avenue South, Nashville, TN 37212. All rights reserved. Used by Permission.

"Reach Out to Jesus" written by Ralph Carmichael. © Copyright 1968, Bud Johns Songs, Inc., 2505 21st
Avenue S., Nashville, TN 37212. All rights reserved. Used by Permission.

"The Wreck of the Edmund Fitzgerald" written by Gordon Lightfoot. © Copyright 1976, Moose Music,
Inc. Used by permission.

"Where Everybody Knows Your Name" written by Gary Portnoy and Judy Hart Angelo. © Copyright
1982 by Addax Music Co., Inc.

Excerpts from *The Spirit of the Disciplines* by Dallas Willard. © Copyright 1989 by Dallas Willard.
Reprinted by permission of HarperCollins Publishers.

"The Wanderer" written by Ernest Maresca. © Copyright 1960, MIJAC MUSIC. All rights administered by
Warner-Tamerland Publishing Corporation. All rights reserved. Used by permission.

"Tie a Yellow Ribbon Round the Ole Oak Tree" written by Irwin Levine and L. Russell Brown.
© Copyright 1973 by Levine and Brown Music. All rights administered by Peermusic Ltd., International.
Copyright secured. All rights reserved. Used by permission.

"Mansion Over the Hilltop" written by Ira Stanphill. © Copyright 1949, Singspiration Music ASCAP. All
rights reserved. Used by Permission. Benson Music Group, Inc.

Excerpts from *The Edge of Adventure* by Bruce Larson and Keith Miller, © Copyright 1974, Word, Inc.;
used by permission.

Editor: Gwen Weising

Cover illustration: Jeff Stoddard

Book designer: Jeff Stoddard

Printed in the United States of America

92 93 94 95 96 97/10 9 8 7 6 5 4 3 2 1

To Tammy

Table of Contents

Dedication   v

Foreword   viii

Acknowledgements   xi

BEGINNINGS

1. As We Begin Our Journey   1
2. Quiet Desperation   5
3. Dangers Yet Unknown   15

FOUNDATIONS

4. Gifts   27
5. The Sins of the Father   41
6. The Gift of Stability   49
7. The Gift of Example   61
8. The Gift of Faith   67
9. The Gift of Freedom   79

THE JOURNEY

10. Starting Over/ Letting Go   87
11. New Foundations   101
12. Something to Believe In   115
13. Every Step of the Way   125
14. Cheers   137
15. Real People   149

THE DESTINATION

16. Dead End   169
17. The Day I Died   185
18. Profile of a Saint   201
19. There's a Light in the Window   215
20. Come Before Winter   223

Acknowledgements

I would sincerely like to thank the following who've stood beside me.

My entire family at Christ Community Church, especially my elder board: Jeff DeVaney, Deb Isle, Hope Lindman, Marilyn Lundgren, Bob Sheplee, Dan Schulist, and Dan Wilson. And much love to Tom and Deb Isle who have been there to remind me that "love is a choice."

To Drs. Robert Hemfelt, Frank Minirth and Paul Meier for your book *Love Is a Choice*. The roller coaster ride to recovery, although painful, is far more thrilling than the ferris wheel of denial.

To Glen Larson and Dr. Steve, thanks.

To Bill and Brian at Olmstead's, thanks for your love, and I can't forget the submarine sandwiches.

Hey, Marty, how can I say thanks?

Nick, Jan, and Pat...we've been through much together, and our love continues to grow. All three of you mean so very much to me.

Dear Seth, Luke, Jessica, and Zachary, you know how much I love you. Please forgive me for being gone so much. Thanks for all your hugs and kisses, although sometimes I wonder if I deserve them.

And Tammy. What can I say? You have always been there holding me up and I've often taken you for granted. Please don't give up on me.

Finally, if there is any acknowledgment for this book, it must go to Jesus who has been so patient. I love Him because He first loved me.

Foreword

Someone had said, "Joy is the surest sign of the presence of God." If it's true, then Guy Doud's life is full of God's presence. He is extraordinary in spite of, or perhaps because of, his ordinary background and all of the problems that beset him in his early life. According to his own story, those problems covered every base: emotional, relational, psychological, and social.

Nevertheless, his book powerfully demonstrates his joy in the journey. As I read the book, I was struck by the thought that Guy Doud embodies the level of spiritual evolution that God has in mind for His children.

We are all presently living at one of three levels. We are born at the feeling level. We do what feels good and we avoid anything that feels bad. This is all too apparent in young children who cry for what they want and have tantrums when they are thwarted. Many people never change though they find subtler and cleverer ways to get their way. But, however good or bad their outward personna, whether they are thugs or Sunday School teachers, they are motivated by self interest and they do only what feels good.

Most people move beyond the feeling level to the conscience level. They recognize that there is a God, that there are moral values, the Golden Rule and the Ten Commandments, and they try to conform to them. Religion speaks to people at this level, urging them to try harder, to be good and to be concerned for others. But the "oughts" of life can be burdensome and can choke out our joy.

The third level is the level of grace. To abandon ourselves to a God who loves us unconditionally, and who has promised to take care of our past, present, and future sins, is to move into a new dimension. That's the level at which I perceive Guy Doud to be. He made the remarkable discovery that, as God's child, he is an heir to the universe. He is able to give himself away generously and with unquenchable joy.

He makes us all envious. I hope this book will produce an ever increasing tribe of Guy Rice Douds.

Bruce Larson
Co–pastor Crystal Cathedral
Garden Grove, California

Beginnings

As We Begin Our Journey

o you know any saints?" I've been having fun the last few days asking people that question. I've enjoyed their comments:

"They're all dead...died a long time ago..."

"I've seen statues of them in our church."

"I think Mother Teresa is one."

"My mother...she was a saint."

"Never known any..."

Saints. You know, those people to whom Jesus gives abundant life. You know, God's redeemed people, and if you've acknowledged Jesus Christ and know Him as Savior—YOU'RE A SAINT!

One of the best known promises of Jesus Christ is also one of the first verses I ever memorized. (Mostly because it's so short.)

"I came that they might have life, and might have it abundantly (John 10:10 NAS).

Take a quick look around. Right now. What do you see? Do you see many people really experiencing the abundant life? I just have to know. Are YOU a saint? Are YOU experiencing the abundant life?

What's that? What about me, Guy Doud, you ask?

Well, you might already know a little about me if you read my first book *Molder of Dreams*. This book, the one you're reading now, is really the rest of the story.

This is not an autobiography.

It's not a self-help book.

It's not a book of religious instruction.

Well, what kind of book is it, then?

It's a book of confession. It's a book about the homeward journey of a wayward saint—me. You see, it has taken me almost forty years to really believe that God intended the abundant life for me. The verse, after all, says Jesus came so that *they* might have abundant life. It would have helped clear things up if the red letters had read, "I have come so that you, Guy Doud, (or you, dear reader,) might have life, and that you might have it abundantly."

It's like the little kid who learned John 3:16 this way,

"For God so loved ME that He gave His only begotten Son for ME that if I believe in Him I will not perish but will have eternal life."

If little children first learned John 3:16 this way, maybe more of them would grow up really believing what it says. Maybe then we'd have a few more saints.

If little children learned... Ah—there's the rub! If little children learned. That's what this book's about—what little children learn—what Guy Doud learned. What we all learn and then have to unlearn and relearn a new way.

The growth into sainthood is growth into the fullness of abundant life. It begins in the home when we are little children, and it is lived out in the context of the community of believers.

Abundant life as a saint doesn't happen all at once, it is a lifelong journey.

I'm going on now. Won't you come along?

Quiet Desperation

She was gone again. Her attendance was abysmal.

"Does anyone know why Kris is absent so much?" I asked. Most of the students in my class looked up from their writing, but some didn't bother. It was really an unfair question to ask them. I should have asked her counselor. No one responded.

That was April 1986. In only a few days my wife Tammy and I would be standing in the Oval Office. I would be receiving the award as National Teacher of the Year, recognized from the more than 2.5 million public school teachers in this country. But as I looked at my students that day, I felt very undeserving of the honor.

The bell rang, the hour was over. The students rose like cattle at the call.

"Have a good day," I said. Not very original.

Some students answered with "Bye, Mr. Doud," and "See ya," but most were just anxious to get out of the classroom and cruise the halls.

One girl stopped at my desk. "You asked about Kris..." She was hesitant.

5

"Yeah," I said. "What's going on with her?"

The way she looked at me told me two things. She trusted me and she cared about her friend. "I think Kris is an alcoholic. She has blackouts all the time. She's pretty bad."

"Do her parents know?" I asked.

"They're divorced. She lives with her mom, but her mom even lets her drink at home. Her mom's an alcoholic, too."

"That's child abuse," I said.

"Kris isn't a child." The girl seemed almost angry. "She's almost eighteen."

"You're right. Have you or any of your friends tried to encourage her to get some help?" I asked.

"It doesn't do any good." After a pause she continued, "I'm afraid she is going to kill herself with her drinking."

"We've got to help her bottom out," I said. And then I asked, "Do you think you and some of your friends would be willing to get together and confront Kris about her problem?"

"I don't know." Now she seemed frightened.

"If we could help her see herself—hold up a mirror—maybe it would help her face the truth," I said.

"I'll think about it. I've gotta go." She started for the door.

I followed. "I want to talk with Kris's counselor about this. Do you mind?"

"Don't tell him that I told you," she said.

"I thought maybe you'd come talk to him with me." She was surprised.

"I don't want to get Kris in trouble, I just want her to get some help," she said nervously.

"She's already in trouble, and you're one of the people who can see that she gets the help she needs."

"I'll talk to you tomorrow. I've just gotta go." She joined the mass of students surging down the hall and was gone.

The next day I sat at my desk viewing my class. Kris's seat was empty. So was her friend's. But Jill was there—one of the happy ones. Thanks, Jill, for all the smiles.

There was Mark—responsible, mature, and a class leader. He wore a tie beneath his red sweater. He'd been accepted at an Ivy League school for the next year.

Jeff—long blond hair, blue jeans and a T-shirt. He was always polite. An average student. I taught his sister, Bev, some time back. They're a lot alike. Jeff's had a hard time. A few weeks earlier his father had committed suicide. Jeff sits in a kind of daze.

Steve—all sports. Walk, talk, sleep, eat, drink, dream, dress sports.

And Chip—just back to school after being released from an adolescent mental health center where he'd been treated for suicidal tendencies. His face looked as suicidal then as it had the month before. Maybe more so. One question Chip asked me still haunts me: "Why am I the way I am? I don't want to be this way. Why did God make me the way I am?"

One day after school, I talked with Chip. I knew he'd been attending a Christian youth group at one of the local churches. It was some of the other kids in his group who told me about Chip's deep depression. Although he had asked Christ into his life, he still felt hopelessly depressed.

Other people, besides me, also talked to Chip. We told him he was special. He *didn't* believe it. We told him God loved him. He *couldn't* believe it. We told him God wanted to give him an abundant life. He *wouldn't* believe it.

Within weeks after returning to school, Chip was back in a residential treatment center and was again threatening suicide. All of us close to Chip prayed each day for his healing. We didn't want or need another suicide. Our school was still in shock from the suicide deaths of two other students. The words of Michael W. Smith's song "Friends" had become the school song for those who cared. The words of "Friends" have so much meaning.

Packing up the dream God planted
In the fertile soil of you.
I can't believe the hopes He's granted
Means a chapter in your life is through.
We'll keep you close as always,
It won't even seem you've gone,
'Cause our hearts in big and small ways,
Will keep the love that keeps us strong.

Chorus:
And friends are friends forever,
If the Lord's the Lord of them.
And a friend will not say never
'Cause the welcome will not end.
Tho' it's hard to let you go
In the Father's hands we know,
That a lifetime's not too long
To live as friends.

With the faith and love God's given,
Springing from the hope we know,
We will pray the joy you live in
Is the strength that now you show.
We'll keep you close as always,
It won't even seem you've gone,

'Cause our hearts in big and small ways
Will keep the love that keeps us strong.

Why did those students commit suicide? Was life really that bad?

Chip's question kept ringing in my ears, Why did God make me the way I am? Had God made Chip the way he was? Was God responsible for Chip's depression? If God wasn't responsible, why had He allowed it? Why didn't God just wave a magic wand and make everyone happy?

I had asked the question myself. *"Why am I the way I am?"* Even though I was about to go to the White House and receive America's highest honor awarded a teacher, deep within myself I did not have the answer. Beneath my mask of self-assurance, still lived an afraid and insecure, trembling child.

Someone has said that we are the sum of our collective experiences. That sounds quite clinical until those collective experiences are delineated. Our collective experiences begin when we are born into families. We do not live in isolation from the rest of the world. Early in our lives we find it necessary to begin to play a part in the drama of life.

First we learn to interact with our families. Then the drama begins to be complicated as we interact with more and more people. The plot thickens when we enter school. We either form friendships or we fail to form friendships. Here in the early years of our lives we begin to compare ourselves with others. We're richer than some, poorer than others. Smarter than some, less intelligent than others. More handsome than some, less beautiful than others. Popular, unpopular. Lost in the crowd, the center of attention. Teacher's pet, the class scapegoat. The list goes on and on and on.

We form beliefs about ourselves that become our foundations. Our beliefs are usually acted out as behaviors. Behaviors bring consequences that only confirm our beliefs. It's hard to change a belief that is grounded in a lifetime of learning.

"Come on now, put your finger in the fire. You won't be burned," I coax you.

"You're crazy!" you shout.

"No, honestly! I know that once the fire burned you, but it won't any more. Come on, now. Try it. It won't burn. I promise." I try to be my most convincing.

"Forget it! I'm not stupid. Fire burns. Always has, always will!" I can't convince you to change your behavior because of your beliefs.

◆

It's hard to change a belief that is grounded in a lifetime of learning.

◆

In many cases our beliefs are dead set—unchangeable—because they're based on firsthand experience. We know what we know. The tragedy is this: many of our childhood beliefs are *dead wrong,* yet we continue to believe them. We carry these false beliefs throughout our lifetime and right to the grave.

Have you ever been a part of this conversation?

"You're special," someone says to you and really means it.

"No, I'm not," you answer, because that's what you truly believe.

"Yes, you are. You are fearfully and wonderfully made. You're made in God's image. It's in the Bible."

"Then God must be as mixed up as I am, because I'm really a rather insignificant player in this drama called life."

How many people feel like this? Chip for one. He can't believe he really matters. A lifetime of learning has convinced him otherwise.

So here's the challenge. How do you change beliefs that are so fundamental and so deeply rooted that they are wrapped around your very soul? Should you change? What should you believe? Whom should you believe? Should you believe the church? A church? If so, which one? Should you believe the media? Or should you believe the prophets of self-gratification and the gurus of materialistic existentialism? Why don't you find a god who doesn't require much? Let yourself off the hook.

Just what is God's expectation for you, anyhow? "I came that they [you] might have life, and might have it abundantly" (John 10:10).

That's one of God's expectations for you—abundant life!

But then there's Chip and Kris and Josh and a whole society of wayward saints. Census figures show that on any given day, an average of 227,900 Americans are living in a mental health facility. More than a quarter of a million people! According to the United Nations World Health Organization, the most pressing medical problem in the world is not heart disease, not cancer, not malnutrition, but DEPRESSION.

I write from firsthand experience. I've met the demon named "Depression" and we've gone fifteen rounds. Much of my life has been lived in the quiet desperation resulting from chronic depression.

"Quiet desperation." I first heard those words in Mr. Ray Frisch's American Literature class at Brainerd State Junior College in 1971. We were studying Thoreau and I really got into it. I can still hear Professor Frisch as he quoted Thoreau, "The mass of men live lives of quiet desperation." And then he asked, "What does that mean, class?"

I was the first to answer: "It means most people aren't very happy."

"Do you believe that?" Mr. Frisch asked.

No one answered.

Later in a philosophy class, another teacher talked about existentialism, a belief which says nothing is timeless or unchanging; man is what he makes of himself; man is responsible for what he makes of himself; life is meaningless unless meaning can be found, but since nothing is eternal, what has real value?

Quiet desperation. Silent screams. Lonely voices. Haunting cries. I wanted to sing, "I've got the joy, joy, joy, joy down in my heart," and I wanted to mean it.

When I was in high school I received a copy of the following reading:

I'M SPECIAL

I'm special.

In all the world there is nobody like me.
Since the beginning of time, there has never been
another person like me.
Nobody has my smile.
Nobody has my eyes, my nose, my hair, my hands, my voice.

I'm special.

No one can be found who has my handwriting.
Nobody anywhere has my tastes for food or music or art.
No one sees things just as I do.
In all of time there's been no one who laughs like me,
no one who cries like me.
And what makes me laugh and cry will never provoke identical
laughter and tears from anyone else, ever.

No one reacts to any situation just as I would react.

I'm special.

I'm the only one in all of creation who has my set of abilities.
Oh, there will always be somebody who is better at one of
the things I'm good at, but no one in the universe can reach
the quality of my combination of talents, ideas, feelings,
and abilities.
Like a room full of musical instruments, some may excel alone,
but none can match the symphony sound when all are played
together.

I'm a symphony.

Through all of eternity no one will ever look, talk, walk,
think, or do like me.

I'm special. I'm rare.

And, in all rarity, there is great value. Because of
my great rare value, I need not attempt to imitate.
I will accept—yes, celebrate—my differences.

I'm special.

And I'm beginning to realize it's no accident that I'm
special. I'm beginning to see that God made me special
for a very special purpose.
He must have a job for me that no one else can do as well as I.
Out of all the billions of applicants, only one is qualified,
only one has the right combination of what it takes.
That one is me, because...

I'm special.

—Anonymous

I wish I could have really believed that. Maybe then I could have done more to help Chip.

Most books I've read get to this point and then give you, the reader, some answers. Until recently I didn't haven't any answers.

Now, twenty-five years after graduating from junior college, I know a few things. One of the things I know is that *there are no easy answers—no quick fixes.* I also know you must *never* give up.

Another thing I've learned is why I am the way I am, or rather, why I was the way I was. It is possible to change. It is possible to sing, "I've got the joy and the love and the peace of Jesus down in my heart," and really mean it.

I've also learned that the journey is worth all the valleys, all the pain we encounter. Ray Frisch, my American Literature teacher, is still teaching. I wonder if he still makes his students memorize another of Thoreau's famous sayings: "If a man does not keep pace with his companions, perhaps it is because he hears a different drummer. Let him step to the music which he hears, however measured or far away."

Hear Him—a different drummer? He's marking time waiting for you. His beat leads down the road of abundant life. His name is Jesus. The masses of desperate people won't follow Him. Will you?

Listen.

Hear it?

"Follow Me!" He commands.

Dangers Yet Unknown

I pulled the big, green 1954 Buick Special onto Highway U.S. 10 and headed east out of Staples toward Motley. My grandpa's car, Betty, practically knew the way to the Brainerd State Junior College 30 miles away where I was just beginning my sophomore year. We'd been back and forth many times.

The car was a tank, but I felt like a prince driving her, sitting tall behind the huge steering wheel. Even though Grandpa Guy had been gone for two years, I could still smell his Peerless pipe tobacco every time I sat in the driver's seat, and his memory was with me.

Betty's only power steering came from me. I would summon extra strength from my 330-pound frame as I made a turn at a stoplight. Betty didn't have power steering, but she did have a pedal starter. To start the car, all I had to do was step on the gas pedal. I loved playing a trick on my friends. Pretending I could perform magic, I would say, "Abracadabra, Mally Madoo. Make this car start, and right now, too!" While my arms were folded across my chest, Betty would "magically" start.

"How did you do that?" a friend would ask.

"Magic," I replied.

"Oh, sure." Most of my friends were not believers.

Then I would demonstrate the pedal ignition.

"That's cool," they'd respond with some sincerity.

"Isn't that cool?" I would reiterate.

"Yeah, that's neat." Their intonation suggested their enthusiasm was beginning to wear thin.

"I really like it," I would say. And that's where the conversation usually ended. Occasionally, however, one of my friends would get as excited about Betty's pedal start as I was and would bring one of his friends to have me demonstrate my unique magical talent. I especially enjoyed playing the trick on girls, because it usually took them a little longer to catch on and so their enthusiasm also lasted longer. This, in turn, allowed me extra time center stage, which I relished.

Another feature missing from Betty was a radio. Grandma and Grandpa just didn't see the need for one. As I think about it, I realize that even if they'd had a radio they probably couldn't have heard it anyhow. They both wore hearing aids. I remember them adjusting their hearing aids trying to catch what was being said. If too many people were talking at the same time, Grandpa had the habit of turning his hearing aid completely off. You knew when it was off because he'd just sit there with a smile on his face.

A teenager, though, needs sound in a car—a radio, at least. So I rigged up a sound system in Betty. I bought a black, plastic speaker about the size of a shoe box and fastened it up under the dash where the radio should have been. The sound came through fine since the dash was hollow and looked like a screen window with lots of tiny little holes. In fact, as you looked at the perforated dashboard you could see the speaker sitting there behind it. Then I took the speaker wire and attached it to a Craig tape recorder that my sister, Nicki, had given me when I graduated from Staples High School in 1971. Now, all that I needed was a cassette tape.

My favorite was a tape of Elvis Presley singing Gospel music. My favorite Elvis Gospel song was "Reach Out to Jesus." He sang it as only Elvis could:

Is your burden heavy, as you bear it all alone?
Does the road you travel harbor danger yet unknown?
Are you growing weary in the struggle of it all?
Jesus will help you when on His name you call.

I'd join Elvis on the chorus:

He is always there, hearing every prayer,
Faithful and true;
Walking by our side, in His love we hide
All the day through.

When you get discouraged just remember what to do—
Reach out to Jesus, He's reaching out to you.

Elvis would sing the last line several times, repeating "reach out to Jesus, reach out to Jesus, reach out to Jesus" and I—singing along—would more than double his volume. I had put a "Honk if you love Jesus" bumper sticker on the back fender of Betty, but if another car had been honking at me, I could not have heard it over the duet Elvis and I were singing. I'm sure people in the cars that passed must have heard and seen me performing and thought I had gone crazy. I not only sang, but I threw my head back and made facial expressions appropriate to the words I was singing. I wasn't driving a car. I was on stage with Elvis! The audience was filled with lost, longing souls and I wanted them to know that what they needed to do was to *"reach out to Jesus."*

I remember that September day when I first parked Betty at Brainerd State Junior College. She was the oldest car in the lot, but also the proudest. I sat behind the big wheel for a few moments before going into the school. This was college, and I was petrified.

I had confided this fear to some trusted adults. They all said, "You're really a good boy, Guy. You have everything you need to succeed. You'll do just fine in college."

But couldn't they see what I really feared?

I turned Elvis off. Other students were parking around me and getting out of their cars and entering the classroom building. They all looked so confident, so beautiful, so handsome. I hoped to see just one other 300-pounder, but everyone looked like Ali MacGraw or Ryan O'Neil. Skinny! Gorgeous!

Minnesota often saves its last blast of summer heat for the start of the school year. This year was no exception. It was hot. I was perspiring profusely. My shirt was already drenched, and the sweat from my forehead ran into my eyes. I searched the car for something to wipe off the sweat, but, finding nothing, I started toward the men's room in the classroom building to get a paper towel. I said good-bye to Betty and Elvis, grabbed my briefcase, and took that first step toward college.

One of the first things I learned in college was that students didn't carry briefcases. And was I the only one in a polyester leisure suit and tie? Didn't anyone else like Elvis?

All the other students seemed to be talking with friends. They all seemed to know each other. Was I the only stranger? I got that familiar sick feeling in my stomach, the same one that in my junior year of high school caused me to come home from Boy's State after only two days, the same one that caused me to come home after only one hour of kindergarten.

I stood still, confused about what to do until I saw signs directing freshmen to the registrar's office. There was hope. I was assigned an advisor and I went to meet with him. The perspiration was flowing even more profusely now.

Mr. Robert Dryden, my advisor, greeted me with a genuine smile and shook my hand. He remembered me, he said, because he had judged the District 24 High School One-Act Play Contest where I had received the Best Actor award. "I hope you plan on being in our theater program," he said.

"I hope I can," I answered, wondering if I would be good enough to get a part, wondering, too, if I would be able to survive college. "Tryouts for our first play begin tomorrow night. Please come." Then Mr. Dryden explained the theater program and it was obvious he was excited about it and was actively recruiting people to be a part of it. He got especially excited when he talked about the new theater building. "It doesn't even have seats in it yet. Would you like to see it?"

"I'd love to," I said.

He gave me the complete tour and I was impressed. The facility included a make-up room, a sound booth, an orchestra pit, a scene shop, and all theatrical necessities. Compared to the gymnasium at Staples High School where I was used to performing, this place was Carnegie Hall!

As we walked across the stage I imagined myself starring in a play, for once playing the leading man instead of the heavy. I could almost hear the women in the audience crying, and as the lights go down on the final scene (where I am dying in my true love's arms), the audience immediately stands to its feet with thunderous applause.

"Do you think you are going to be able to try out tomorrow night?" Mr. Dryden's voice ended my fantasy.

"I think so," I said, now pretty excited about the possibility of being in a college play.

I remember my first play quite well. It was called *A Company of Wayward Saints* and was about a Commedia Dell'Arte troupe of traveling actors. Commedia Dell'Arte is a form of Italian comedy that originated in the Middle Ages. In Commedia Dell'Arte actors would improvise dialogue and action around outline plots. Each play had stock characters. I played the part of Capitano, who, of course, was the heavy.

Little did I know then that this was not just a role. I did not know that I, too, was a wayward saint.

◆

I know that it is in the ordinary circumstances, the boring, the longitude and latitude of life, that our faith either works or it doesn't. It is in the day-to-day experiences where we either enjoy the abundant life or we don't.

◆

My role in *A Company of Wayward Saints* was followed by a role in Rodgers and Hammerstein's *Oklahoma*. Once again I played the heavy, Judd Fry. I played numerous other roles for Bob Dryden, but my favorite was as the Stage Manager in Thornton Wilder's classic drama, *Our Town*. At one time *Our Town* was required reading for most high school American Literature students. Somehow I had graduated from high school never having been exposed to this drama.

I couldn't wait each evening for the cue from the real stage manager to walk out on stage and look at the audience and say, "This play is called *Our Town*. It was written by Thornton Wilder; produced and directed by Mr. Bob Dryden." It seemed like such a practical way to begin a play. Mr. Dryden told me to deliver the lines "as though you're talking to people in your living room. Be conversational," he said. "Be as comfortable as an old shoe."

And then the Stage Manager, who serves as the narrator of the play, listed others in the cast and continued: "The name of this town is Grover's Corner, New Hampshire, just across the Massachusetts line: latitude 42 degrees 40 minutes, longitude 70 degrees 37 minutes. The first act shows a day in our town. The day is May 7, 1901. The time is just before dawn."

I remember when I first read those lines from the script to *Our Town* I thought, *How boring. Who cares what a town's latitude and longitude is, anyhow?* I know now that it is in the ordinary circumstances, the boring, the longitude and latitude of life, that our faith either works or it doesn't. It is in the day-to-day experiences where we either enjoy the abundant life or we don't. It is in the routine daily activities where we are called to live out our sainthood. We must capture what we've thought trivial and live as "saints in the light."

I slowly walked out on stage to start the third act of each performance. The act takes place in the cemetery, and as it begins the Stage Manager explains that nine years have passed since the end of Act Two, which ended with the marriage of Emily Webb and George Gibbs.

I, as the Stage Manager, walked out as the lights came up and said: "Nineteen, thirteen. Gradual changes in Grover's Corners.

Horses are getting rarer. Farmers coming into town in Fords. Everybody locks their house doors now at night. Ain't been any burglars in town yet, but everybody's heard about 'em."

As I said those lines in the comfortable, conversational manner, I slowly walked across stage before stopping to say, "This is certainly an important part of Grover's Corners." Then I looked around at the cemetery, pointing out different sections: the older one with its Civil War Veterans and Daughters of the American Revolution; the newer one where those from the first two acts were now "buried."

There are no tombstones in this play; instead, Wilder has the actors sit bolt upright in chairs, staring straight ahead into the audience. We recognize George's mother, Mrs. Gibbs, and Simon Stimson, the alcoholic organist from the Congregational Church, among others.

Each night as I performed this role I couldn't help but think of visiting the Staples cemetery and the graves of my grandparents. Now, twenty years later, I go there to visit both of my parents' graves and graves of many of the people I told you about in *Molder of Dreams*. Yeah, each year Evergreen Hill becomes a more familiar place. I often think about what an old man I visited in the nursing home said to me: "I have more friends in Evergreen Hill than anywhere else. I want to join them." He was ready to go.

But Emily wasn't. Remember now, Emily is the young girl who got married to George Gibbs at the end of Act Two. Not long into Act Three a funeral procession stops at an imaginary grave where four men lower an invisible casket.

One of dead women asks "Who is it, Julia?" And Julia Gibbs responds: "My daughter-in-law, Emily Webb."

"What did she die of, Julia?"

"In childbirth."

"Childbirth. I'd almost forgotten all about that. My, wasn't life awful and wonderful?"

Soon the live people who've come for the committal begin to sing "Blessed Be the Tie That Binds," and as they sing, Emily appears, walking slowly toward the dead people sitting in their chairs. After watching them for a while, Emily asks her mother-in-law: "Live people don't understand, do they?"

And Mother Gibbs responds: "No, dear, not very much."

Emily says, "Oh, Mother Gibbs, I never realized before how troubled and how...how in the dark live persons are. From morning till night, that's all they are—troubled."

I would stand off to the side each night and watch as Carla Bayerl from Pierz, Minnesota, who played the part of Emily, looked back and forth between the living and the dead, not sure with whom she belonged. I agonized with her. Each evening Carla would approach me as Emily does the Stage Manager and would ask for the chance to go back and live life over again. The Stage Manager tells her that if she goes back she'll not only live, but watch herself live and she'll know the future, what happens next. He explains to her that it is far too painful and advises her to take her place among the dead. But she insists and wants to go back and relive the day she first realized that she loved George. Mother Gibbs advises against picking that day and says, "Choose the least important day in your life. It will be important enough."

Finally, Emily decides to relive her twelfth birthday, and so the Stage Manager takes her back fourteen years. She suddenly sees Main Street of Grover's Corners and is amazed to see people walking down the street whom she knows are dead. It's the town she knew as a little girl. She can't believe how much she's forgotten. She sees the white fence that used to be around her childhood home and suddenly realizes that she loved that fence, but she'd forgotten all about it. She stands outside her house and asks the

Stage Manager if her parents are inside, and he tells her yes. Soon she is a child again and her mother is in the kitchen fixing breakfast. Emily is amazed at how young her parents look. She can't remember them ever looking that young. She is overcome with a hundred different emotions, but her mother tells her to sit down and "chew your bacon good and slow."

Emily can't understand why her mother doesn't look at her. She pleads with her mother who can't hear her, "Oh, Mama, just look at me one minute as though you really see me. Mama, fourteen years have gone by; I'm dead. You're a grandmother, Mama, I'm married to George Gibbs. Mama, Wally's dead, too. Mama, his appendix burst on a camping trip to North Conway. We felt just terrible about it—don't you remember? But, just for a moment now we're all together. Mama, just for a moment we're happy. Let's look at one another."

But Mama goes about her kitchen duties. Emily breaks down, sobbing, and turns to the Stage Manager who has been witnessing the entire scene: "I can't go on. It goes so fast. We don't have time to look at one another. I didn't realize all that was going on and we never noticed."

Then Emily asks to be taken back to the grave, but first she takes one last look at Grover's Corners and says, "Good-bye. Good-bye, world. Good-bye, Grover's Corners...Mama and Papa. Good-bye to clocks ticking...and Mama's sunflowers. And food and coffee. And new-ironed dresses and hot baths...and sleeping and waking up. Oh, earth, you're too wonderful for anybody to realize you."

Emily looks directly at the Stage Manager. She asks, "Do any human beings ever realize life while they live it—every, every minute?"

Each night that question sent a shiver down my spine. I would look at Carla, our Emily, and try to answer her as matter-of-factly as possible, "No. The saints and poets, maybe—they do some."

Returning to the grave Emily tells Mother Gibbs, "I should have listened to you. That's all humans are! Just blind people."

I hated to see the run of *Our Town* come to an end. I had learned a lot. There are no unimportant days or unimportant events. It's like the beginning of this chapter. I'd forgotten all about listening to Elvis and how I used to sing along with him until I started writing this chapter. Life can be awful, and wonderful. It depends, I believe, on whether or not we reach out to Jesus who's reaching out to us. "Do humans realize life while they live it?" Saints do! Saints do!

But maybe, like Emily, we've taken a lot of life for granted. If only we could all go back and see what we've missed.

What is it that keeps us from knowing God's abundance and living like saints?

◆

I believe that if Christians were convinced of their sainthood and lived like saints, joy would be bursting out all over the place. Think of it!

◆

We have been born with a sin nature, which is basically our desire to put self before God. It is this nature that blinds us to beauty and keeps us from knowing the abundance Christ has promised us.

We must also remember we face active opposition from an enemy who delights in making life seem awful. His name is Satan. He is not the childhood image I had of a man in a funny red suit with horns and a pitchfork who is trying to keep Santa Claus from delivering his Christmas presents. He is instead the number one stealer of our joy. Scripture warns us, "Be self-controlled and alert. Your enemy the devil prowls around like a roaring lion looking for someone to devour" (1 Pet. 5:8).

Satan "devours" us by convincing us that "there must be more to life than this." So we try this and experiment with that. We forsake the faith of childhood and abandon our families. We throw out the Ten Commandments and God's moral imperatives and we get caught in one or more of Satan's many traps, until life has rushed by and we realize we've never lived.

This book is for all of us who want to live and experience the abundance of life. To be honest, I'm still learning how to do it. Despite accepting Christ in junior high school, I'm just learning what it truly means to reach out to Jesus.

I believe that if Christians were convinced of their sainthood and lived like saints, joy would be bursting out all over the place. Think of it!

God helped me make it through those first few days and weeks of college. Even now, years later, I can see how so many seemingly unimportant events from those days have influenced who I am and what I have become.

The freshman in the polyester leisure suit carrying the big briefcase was pretty naive. He had many things to learn about himself. He didn't know, yet, just how much he needed the touch of Christ. As he headed home tugging at the wheel of the '54 Buick he called Betty, Elvis sang from inside his dash,

> *Is the life you're living filled with sorrow and despair?*
> *Does the future press you with its worry and its care?*
> *Are you tired and friendless, have you almost lost your way?*
> *Jesus will help you, just come to Him today.*

Foundations

s I sit here writing I'm looking out at Lake Superior. It's a bright, sunny morning, all the more appreciated because it follows two weeks of fog, rain, and snow. Funny, in just two weeks I'd forgotten how spectacular a sunny day can be.

Even though it's January, there is still open water and there are still boats on the lake. Back home in Brainerd the locals and the tourists have been driving on the frozen lakes for several weeks. There's no open water there.

Whole communities of fish houses have been erected on the thick ice of the lakes near Brainerd. According to the Minnesota Department of Natural Resources there are over 6,400 fish houses on Mille Lacs Lake alone. That's more houses than in many Minnesota towns.

Some of the fish houses are portable and can only seat one fisherman, but I've seen some bigger than my boyhood home, some with two and even three stories. Yeah, around these parts there are people who are crazy about ice fishing. Come winter, fishing becomes life to them. They cast any other form of life aside and live to fish. They stay in their fish houses for days. I've heard that some lakes even erect road signs, although I've never seen them, and I've heard that one of these ice cities elects a mayor, a town council, and a town constable who all delight in doing nothing but fishing.

Someday I'm going to do it, too. Fish that is. I don't think I'll ever want to actually live in a fish house, but I would like to try ice fishing. People can't believe it when I tell them I've lived here all my life and I've never gone ice fishing.

Seth and Luke, my two oldest sons, have been bugging me to take them ice fishing, but I told them I don't know how to go about it. Where do you get the house? How do you know where to drill the hole? What do you use for bait? Where do you learn these things, anyhow? I guess most of the fishermen learned all about ice fishing when they were kids. The skills were passed on to them and they, in turn, passed on the knowledge to their kids. Neither my dad or my mom or my grandparents ice fished. None of my sisters or my brother ice fish, and I doubt that my children will become fisherman because neither my wife nor I have ever taught them. Oh, they could teach themselves, but I bet they won't. What do you think?

It's the same way with hunting. I don't know anything about it except that during deer hunting season you better wear a bright orange jacket. In November hunters with rifles slung on their shoulders, big knives attached to their belts, and hungry looks in their eyes, sit in the trees, pretending they're not freezing, waiting for a buck to stroll into their sights. Drive out into the country and listen. It sounds like World War III. Cars and trucks pass through town with legs and hooves sticking out their back ends.

One guy I know seems to be a rather meek, timid man, but

come hunting season he straps his twelve inch knife to his belt, gets out his .30-06, and becomes the Terminator.

I've never hunted, except for rats at the old Staples City Dump. I told you that story in *Molder of Dreams.* My dad never hunted either, and I doubt very much that my children will ever be hunters.

Hobbies like hunting and fishing and family traditions are passed on from generation to generation. Unless something has been a part of your childhood experience, it will probably not become a part of your adult experience. You may not even know you're interested.

It's like our faith. I heard a few years ago that about 90 percent of the people who become Christians do so before the age of twenty-one. The last few years as I've travelled and spoken, I've asked many Christian audiences this question, "How many of you became Christians before age twenty-one?" Most hands go up. "How many of you became Christians after the age of twenty-one?" Usually only a few hands in the crowd are raised. That's why childhood is so important. It provides the foundation on which people build their lives. Unfortunately for many people the foundation is cracked, broken, and deteriorated, but they don't even realize it because they've never known anything else. As far as they know, that's how life is. For this reason many of us grow up never knowing the beauty of life because we've never experienced it in our families. We've never come to know our sainthood. We're wayward saints.

I'm sure there are hundreds of books about hunting and fishing, but I'm not very interested in them. My foundation was built without them and now I don't have the time or the desire to read them. Likewise, there are many great books and tapes available about Christian living. And then there is the Bible itself. Unless reading the Bible and other Christian literature is part of a person's foundation, he probably won't want to read them.

Do you see the importance of childhood foundations?

I told you at the start of this chapter that I'm looking out at Lake Superior. I know that somewhere out there lies the wreck of the *Edmund Fitzgerald*. I can close my eyes and hear in my mind Gordon Lightfoot singing about the Fitzgerald in his haunting ballad:

> *The legend lives on from the Chippewa on down,*
> *to the big lake they call Gitche Gumee.*
> *Superior it says never gives up its dead*
> *'til the gales of November come early.*

I find it hard to believe that this lake, so peaceful today, in a moment of angry fury destroyed that ship and all of its men. This peaceful lake has devoured not only the Fitzgerald, but many other ships as well.

The lake is spectacular. It's a gift. The sunshine today, that's a gift, too.

"Besides God's gift of Himself in the person of Jesus Christ and the power of His Holy Spirit, what is His most special gift?" I ask myself. I quickly answer, "Life itself--the breathing, thinking, feeling, laughing, crying, eating, talking, and walking. That's God's special gift."

The eagle that soars near the Mississippi river just a couple of blocks from where I live is a gift. The squirrel that courageously walks up the stairs of our deck and sits on two legs to eat the bread we've put there for him is a gift. The maple tree that each fall puts on a show like no other in town—what a gift! And I must not forget the whippoorwill who called out so loudly at three in the morning that my neighbor's son finally walked outside and yelled at the top of his lungs, "Shut up!" That noisy whippoorwill is a gift, too. But those are not the only gifts I recall. I also think of the gift of community. Staples, Minnesota, my hometown, gave me the gift of community. Although I've been away from Staples for twenty years, I still feel it.

Each Thursday I receive my weekly copy of the *Staples World* newspaper in the mail. Staples' world is not a large world, but it was the world of my childhood and part of me still lives there. Most of what I am comes from there. Although I joke about it, I enjoy reading the newspaper. I love the news concerning outlying communities like Poplar and Leader. In the section of the paper called simply "Poplar News" I read things like this: "George and Harriet Anderson motored Sunday to Minneapolis where they visited their daughter who is expecting her first baby in March." And stories like this: "Grace and Harold Larson were the Friday evening dinner guests of Ralph and Ileane Swenson. After a dinner of roast duck—which Harold had shot—cards were played and the evening was enjoyed by all."

Just last Thursday the *World* included this article:

> *The town still wants a resident physician. Unless we get one we may send Lon Francisco to some medical school for a short time, so he can finish his studies and get a diploma. Lon has a good knowledge of materia medica so far as it pertains to a horse, and they say a horse and a man are treated in much the same manner.*

I must confess that the above article appeared in a column called "From the Past, 100 Years Ago."

There is a great big part of me that longs for the simplicity of that Staples world. It was a gift to me, too.

Right now a big ship is heading out across Superior. I wonder who's on board. I wonder where it's going. I imagine a thousand different possibilities. Ah, the gifts of wonder and imagination. Special gifts!

You're a gift, too. Do you believe it?

◆

Beside the gift of Himself in Jesus Christ, I am convinced the most important gift God has given us is the gift of family.

◆

Beside the gift of Himself in Jesus Christ, I am convinced the most important gift God has given us is the gift of family. I know that there are those who have no family and there are many others who have survived despite their dysfunctional families. There are those who've learned to fish and hunt although they never did it as kids. And there are those who've come to faith in Christ as adults even though He was never a part of their childhood. But for most people what happens in their family of origin establishes their foundation for the rest of their lives.

What are the gifts a family gives? I'm not a psychologist or a sociologist. I'm a language arts teacher who has known hundreds of students at Brainerd High School where I've been employed since 1975. Each of them is a product of a family and each of them has received the gifts a family gives.

I'm also a pastor, and as such I've counseled hundreds of people.

Most struggle with the same basic problem—a lack of self-worth and an unclear picture of who God is and what role He plays in their lives. They find it very difficult to believe that God really loves *them* and cares for *them* and desires an abundant life for *them*. God, the father figure, is seen more as one who is uninvolved in their lives. They see Him as someone who is waiting to pass judgment, punishment, and condemnation.

The counseling process usually reveals that this lack of self-worth and this unclear picture of God originated in childhood. As much as the counselee would like to have a new picture, he finds his old beliefs deeply ingrained. The basic question he asks is, "How do I change?" He's overcome with guilt because of the feeling of low self-worth and because of the things he does and because he doesn't know how to change. Many counselees are frustrated with prayer and claim that God doesn't hear, or if He hears, He doesn't answer. They've asked God to change them and nothing has happened.

I remember one very obese lady, years ago, who through tears sobbed as she told me, "I've begged God again and again to take away my desire for food, but He hasn't." She went on to reveal that both her parents had died of heart attacks while relatively young. "Both of my parents were very fat," she said, "and when I was growing up I was ashamed of them. I told myself that I would never be fat, not ever. Now look at me...I'm fatter than my mother ever was."

The gifts a family gives. What are they? We've talked about some negative gifts, but there are positive gifts as well. What about self-worth? stability? example? faith? and freedom?

Let's look at the gift of self-worth first. It's the most important gift a family, in particular, parents, can give a child. It's the family that provides the nurture, support, and encouragement a child needs. This nutriment is almost as important as food and shelter. To become a healthy saint, living an abundant life, a child must believe that he is important—that he matters. His thoughts and feelings must be validated. He must be heard. Perhaps nothing convinces a child of his worth more than a parent who is intimately involved in every aspect of his life and listens to him, truly hearing what he says. I can hear Emily Webb Gibbs come back from the grave begging her mother to "just look at me one minute as though you really see me."

I was serving cake and punch at the "Royal Tea," the annual

♦

Perhaps nothing convinces a child of his worth more than a parent who is intimately involved in every aspect of his life and listens to him, truly hearing what he says.

♦

Homecoming reception honoring the newly crowned Brainerd Warrior Homecoming King and Queen and their court. I often joked with my Student Council kids who sponsored the event that it was "the 'Royal Tea' for the royal—ty." Yes, they thought it was a pretty corny joke, too.

"Mr. Doud," a student said, right after I handed her a piece of cake, "can I talk with you for a few moments?"

Although I was very busy, I saw her eyes begging me. "Sure," I said. She was a beautiful girl. Bubbling personality. A big smile. I was soon to be surprised at the pain hidden behind her laughter.

We walked outside into the courtyard of the high school and

sat on one of the benches. On this cold, fall evening we had the courtyard to ourselves.

"What is it, Judy?" I asked.

"You're really going to think this sounds stupid," she said, "but I really wanted to be one of the Homecoming Queen candidates." She checked my eyes before continuing. "You know, my sister was Homecoming Queen a few years ago and my father and mother are always comparing me to her. I never match up. My grades aren't as good. My room isn't as clean. I'm not as pretty. I'm not as popular. I'm clumsy." Tears rolled from her eyes but the rest of her face still seemed to be smiling.

She continued, "I thought that maybe if I could be a Homecoming Queen candidate, or maybe even the Queen, maybe Mom and Dad would be proud of me." Now the smile disappeared and deep anguish distorted her face.

I reached for her hand and squeezed it. "That isn't stupid, Judy. That isn't stupid. All you really want is to know that you matter and that you are important."

I had given her permission to continue, "I thought that maybe if I had been chosen Homecoming Queen, maybe my dad would be proud of me and maybe, maybe..." The pain was so great now that she couldn't continue. Gentle flowing tears had become heavy sobs that shook her entire body.

I squeezed her hand again and after a moment she continued, "I thought that maybe if I had been chosen Homecoming Queen, maybe my dad would be proud of me and maybe he would quit drinking. He's an alcoholic. He's been to treatment, but he's back to drinking again."

It was obvious that she blamed herself for her father's drinking. Subconsciously she believed herself to be responsible for all of the problems in her family. Maybe if her room could be cleaner...if only she could lose a little more weight...maybe if her grades were better...if only she were less clumsy...maybe if she were chosen Homecoming Queen...if only...if only...maybe...maybe then her father would quit drinking and validate her self-worth.

How could I tell her, sitting there in the high school courtyard that cold, September evening, that she was every bit as capable, important, and lovable as her sister? How could I tell her that she in no way was responsible for her father's drinking or for the troubles in her family? How could I tell her that better grades and being Homecoming Queen were not the answer? Whatever I would tell her was contradicted by seventeen years of personal experiences. A long conviction of worthlessness builds strong walls.

Instead of the gift of self-worth, Judy had received a gift of

◆

No other unit of society can take the place of the home and the family. School can't, even though it tries, and the church can't, even though it sometimes thinks it can.

◆

conditional acceptance. She had come to believe that her value was determined by how well she performed and she could never perform well enough to become the Queen. I wondered what she might do to receive the unconditional love for which she was hungering?

When you think of all the Judys there are, it becomes quite obvious why teenage pregnancy and suicide rates keep rising. It's obvious why millions of our youth fall victim to chemical dependency.

They are searching for unconditional love they have not experienced at home.

No other unit of society can take the place of the home and the family. School can't, even though it tries, and the church can't, even though it sometimes thinks it can. God intended that nurturing and the establishment of a good foundation come from the family. There simply is no substitute for a family's unconditional love.

What's ironic about all this is that many of us do not realize we haven't received the gift of self-worth from our parents. Judy would have told you her parents were the most loving parents anyone could have. She felt that if she could only get *her* act together, her family would be happy. She was unable to see the situation truthfully. Her vision was distorted.

The truth is her father was very sick and his sickness infected the entire family. Judy's mother made it possible for her father to keep drinking. She relied on lies and wishful thinking in order to survive his alcoholism.

Judy's older sister, so much more successful than Judy, became a hero child who brought honor to the family and helped keep it functioning. She carried a heavy load. Her younger brother became the family clown as a way of coping. He was a sports nut, who never took anything too seriously.

And then there was Judy. She felt she couldn't do anything right. If only she could, she thought, then all of her family's problems would be solved. The tragedy is that Judy can't see how totally deluded her thinking is, and unless she truly discovers her sainthood by coming to Christ and letting Him fill her longing with His unconditional love, she will spend the rest of her life wishing she were the Queen.

The big ship is gone from my view now. It slid below the horizon of Lake Superior, the "Lake Gitche Gumee."

I make a pot of coffee.

It's getting dark outside. Darkness comes early during Minnesota winters.

The coffee is good. It, too, is a gift. I think about the coffee—it's expensive. And then I think about God's gifts—they're free.

I'm thinking about that and I'm remembering being in my tent in the backyard of my Staples world. I had no idea then how big the world is. This night I'm at its center. It revolves around me. I should be sleeping, but there's so much to think about. So many questions needing answers. Janis Joplin is singing on my portable radio that needs new batteries: "Nothing ain't worth nothing unless it's free." I didn't understand then what that meant. I do now. I go outside the tent. The sky is all stars—gifts.

One star is moving. It's not a star but a satellite, I think. I bet it's a Russian spy satellite and I bet it's spying on me.

I'd forgotten all about my tent and the Russians spying on me until just now. For just a moment I was a kid again and had the opportunity to relive that moment. Memory—it's a gift, too.

But what about things too painful to remember? Aren't there things it would be better to forget? Judy has already forgotten lots of things about her childhood. For some of us forgetting is a necessity, a survival mechanism. I'd forgotten huge chunks about my childhood until very recently when my life started to spin out of control. At that time I was forced to take a look at what was causing my problem. In my search I found myself on the doorstep of my childhood looking in, trying to understand why I had wound up where I was.

I did not come out of childhood with the foundational gift of self-worth. I, even more than Judy, thought my value was directly related to my performance. I've found it necessary to re–learn much of what I learned in childhood. I've had to replace the foun-

dation of conditional acceptance with unconditional love.
It's completely dark outside now. I can't see the lake. There's
just black night that goes on forever. Night is a gift, too. Nighttime—
a chance to rest. I'm going to rest now. How about you?

The Sins of the Father

ou may wish to skip this chapter. It's not a chapter, really, it's more like a letter. It is very personal. Can I trust you to read it?

If you decide to read it, first read this verse. "You shall not bow down to them [idols] or worship them; for I, the LORD your God, am a jealous God, punishing the children for the sin of the fathers to the third and fourth generation of those who hate me" (Ex. 20:5).

Every one called him "Sonny."

I'm looking at a picture taken of him and the softball team he played on in Grand Forks, North Dakota. The picture was taken in 1936. That would make him twenty. Somebody from Grand Forks mailed the picture to me just a month or so ago. He said he thought I should have it. I appreciate it very much.

Half of his teeth are missing. "Sonny probably lost them in a fight," said someone who knew him then. And there's that familiar scar on his cheek. He had it even then.

His black tennis shoes would be right in style today. The

square outline of his face seems strange to me. I remember it as rounded. Sonny was the catcher on the team. A good one I've been told.

It's sad. This is the earliest picture I have of him. In fact, I hardly have any pictures of him. Weren't there any wedding pictures taken after he eloped that New Year's Eve? Or pictures of him holding his newborn babies? Or of him on his birthday or at Christmas? There don't seem to be pictures of his parents either.

There's an angry look in his eyes. It's probably the look that helped him survive the jump at Anzio and many months in a German prisoner of war camp.

Why are you so angry at such an early age, Sonny? What has life dealt you to harden you so?

Everyone called him "Sonny." I called him Dad.

Dad, there's so much I don't know about you. Did you ever know your grandparents? Where were they from? What were their names? In what ways am I like them? What was your mother's maiden name? What was your first wife's name? Was she pretty? Why did you divorce? Ronnie, the son of that marriage died at the age of eight of spinal menningitis. Are there any pictures of my half-brother? Did he look at all like me? I finally found his grave near the part of the cemetery called "Baby Land" in Grand Forks. The stone doesn't mark the day he died, just the year. That must have been a sad day.

What did you do with your pain, Dad?

Did Ronnie know about Jesus? You never talked about Ronnie, Dad.

I couldn't find your parents' grave when I went to look this fall. Snow had already laid a blanket over the earth and I could find no marker that read "Doud." I'll look again come spring. A part of me is buried there that I need to visit if only to say good-bye.

I remember the night I prayed with you, Dad, to receive Jesus into your life. It was one of the happiest moments of my life. And at the funeral home when Joe Brenny, the mortician, asked me if I had anything I wished I had told you I answered "no," and that was the truth then. But I realize that there are a million questions I'd like to ask you now.

◆

We want our children to grow up healthy. We want to give them all the gifts parents can. We want them to know that they are "saints" and live like it, experiencing all the abundance that Christ promised.

◆

Tammy and I have four children Seth, nine; and Luke, eight, both of whom you loved to hold and kiss; and Jessica, five, and Zachary, two, whom you never knew. Jessica, our only girl, holds her own against her brothers. She calls them "my boys." She's really a sweetheart, Dad. You'd enjoy spoiling her. One look at her long eyelashes and blue eyes and you'd melt. And Zachary. What a wild man! He climbs up on the kitchen counter, and when you walk into the kitchen, he leaps at you expecting you to be always ready to catch him. I've never dropped him yet.

We want our children to grow up healthy. We want to give them all the gifts parents can. We want them to know that they are "saints" and live like it, experiencing all the abundance that Christ promised. But I struggle to be a good father, Dad. I find myself doing things and saying things that I always told myself I would never do and say. Many of these things are the things you did.

Most of the time you were uninvolved in my life, You would

come home from work and plant yourself in front of the television or sit in your chair and read a book. Oh, there were a few times you took me swimming and things like that, but those times were few and far between. It's funny, but one of my fondest memories of you is when I'd have an earache—and I had them often—you'd have me sit on your lap. You'd light up one of your cigarettes and blow its smoke into my aching ears. It seemed to help. I'm not sure it was the smoke that helped. Maybe it was just the fact that it felt good to sit there on your lap, the center of your attention.

There are so many things I'd forgotten, hoping that they would just go away. But they scarred me, Dad. When my childhood foundation started to disintegrate, I discovered that I really hadn't forgotten. I began to realize that the only way I could really be healed was to allow Jesus to build a whole new foundation. In order to do that, I had to get rid of the old one. That's why I'm telling you these things.

There was hatred in your eyes when you grabbed your belt and told me you were going to "blister my butt." I can't remember even one of the terrible things I must have done to make you yell that way. But I remember your eyes. I remember the belt. And the profanity. I've cried because I've found myself yelling at Seth and Luke like that, Dad. No matter how much I apologized, the words of apology need to wait for appropriate behavior in order to be believed. Their young souls won't soon forget such harshness. My soul remembers. Is that the way your father punished you? Is that the way your father's father punished him? The sins of the fathers?

I wish I could put this next memory back in the spot where I've kept it hidden for twenty-five years, but that spot doesn't want it any more. Jesus lives there now. So I have to get rid of it—I have to confess it and give it to Him. I'm talking about the pornography, Dad. Your books. I read them. What I read still haunts me. Neither you nor Mom ever explained God's beautiful gift of sex to me. I learned about it from your books. You kept them in your dresser drawer, but I found them. You read them quite openly at night and I would look at the pictures on the covers when I was on my way to bed.

It only took me a few minutes to find them one day when I was home alone. I have never been the same since reading those books. Honestly, Dad, that pornography was a form of sexual abuse. It took away my innocence and distorted my attitude toward sex. The books were as explicit as anything I could imagine. I'm angry, Dad, because you robbed me of learning about sex the way God intended it to be, as the fullest expression of love between a man and wife. I'm still recovering, Dad. Jesus is healing the scars, but I've had to confront them.

I didn't feel sorry for you the night before Mother's funeral. It was the first time I ever saw you cry. You came out of the bedroom and walked up to Nicki, Jan, Pat, and me as we sat at the kitchen table, which had always served as the command center of our home. Mother always sat there. I think all four of us were amazed to see the tears in your eyes. "I never told her that I loved her, but I think she knew." You said that. And it was like you expected us to have sympathy for you. I didn't. I was angry at you. I never saw you and mother hold hands or hug or kiss. After I learned about sex, I wondered if I had been immaculately conceived. I rarely recall either of you having a conversation of any length. You taught me that a wife is a servant who makes your meals, washes your clothes, raises the kids, pays the bills, and is basically responsible for keeping the family running. Is that what your dad taught you?

The truth is, Mom didn't know that you loved her. She told me. "I don't think your father loves me." She said it simply, but then it was as if she expected me to love her all that much more, and I felt guilty that I couldn't give her all the love it was so obvious she needed.

She was starved for love so she looked to all of us kids to find it. I've heard it called "emotional incest" and "smother love." She smothered us with her love as she took tranquilizers to ward off her bouts of depression and anxiety. All she wanted, she said, was for everyone to be happy and get along. Because she wanted it so badly, I wanted it too and felt that if I only worked harder, tried harder, maybe things would go better. I only recently realized, Dad, that I've been trying ever since. But I don't have to do it, I can't do it, anymore.

◆

We've been wayward saints.
But that's why God sent Jesus,
to reconcile us to Him.

◆

You said she spoiled us. You'd get angry at her. I have to admit I thought it pretty great to have a mother who was so totally devoted to her children and who always put our needs ahead of her own. But I never guessed that I would expect that same type of devotion from my wife and feel cheated when I didn't receive it. I was shocked when Tammy told me she felt I expected her to be my mother and that was a role she just couldn't fill. I didn't have to think about it very long before I realized that Tammy was right.

These are some of the main things I've learned, Dad, and I'm not telling you them to blame you or Mom for anything. I think we could trace the blame all the way back to the Garden of Eden when Adam and Eve decided to worship the creature rather than the Creator. Ever since, there's been sin in the world. Ever since, we've been wayward saints. But that's why God sent Jesus, to reconcile us to Him.

I love what Paul says in his letter to the Philippians. It describes the way I feel right now:

> Not that I have already obtained all this, or have already been made perfect, but I press on to take hold of that for which Christ Jesus took hold of me. Brothers, I do not consider myself yet to have taken hold of it. But one thing I do: Forgetting what is behind and straining toward what is ahead, I press on toward the goal to win the prize for which God has called me heavenward in Christ Jesus.
>
> (Phil. 3:12-14)

I press on, Dad. I still have a long way to go on the road to recovery. I think it's like the Christian journey; it never ends. It's like what Paul just said: "Not that I have already obtained all this, or have been made perfect, but I press on." I press on. I've never loved you and Mom more, but I don't want my family to be hurt in the same way I was hurt. The time has come to break the cycle. I forgive you and realize that you probably didn't know how much you hurt me. Nor did Mom know how unhealthy her possessive love was. I forgive you both.

That picture of you in your softball outfit—the one with your teeth missing—I framed it and it sits on my bookshelf now.

I love the way Paul brings his letter to the Philippians to a close. It's a great way to end a letter. He says: "Greet all the saints in Christ Jesus...All the saints send you greetings..." (Phil.4:21,22).

We're saints, Sonny! I want to live like one.

The Gift of Stability

When I had a chance to go back to my alma mater, Concordia College in Moorhead, Minnesota, and address the Education Department, I joked that they hadn't done a very good job teaching me to be a teacher because they had never taught me how to conduct lavatory duty. I've never heard Madeline Hunter or any of the other teaching specialists suggest any lavatory supervision methods either. And I've never been evaluated on lavatory duty so I don't know if I'm doing it right. I just try to follow my principal's basic advice: "Be clearly visible." That isn't too difficult as I'm usually the only one in the toilet wearing a suit.

Almost as frustrating for me as lavatory duty is hall duty. Again the idea is to be visible to ward off potential problems and I guess it works because I've never witnessed any major catastrophies. I'm thankful that my tenure of lavoratory and hall duty has been spent at Brainerd High School in Minnesota. In my travels as National Teacher of the Year, I spoke at one inner city school where they had transformed the high school's sports trophy case into a memorial for students who had been killed in gang-related

49

incidents. It's a long way from that inner city school to Brainerd, Minnesota, and I'm glad! It makes me so very sad to think about what is happening in America. Wayward saints...

I've never witnessed any gang related violence in Brainerd. Oh, we've had some vandalism now and then, and occasionally someone throws eggs at some other person's car, but those incidents are few and far between. Of course there have been those students who were killed in alcohol-related accidents, and all of us who care will forever grieve the memory of our students who gave up on life and committed suicide. But that isn't unique to Brainerd.

I'd rather think of the positive things, such as the fact that almost everyone graduates from high school in Brainerd. I couldn't believe it when I started to travel and found that over 30 percent of all students in America never graduate from high school. Thirty percent! And most of the ones who do not graduate come from families where their parents didn't graduate either, and then they in turn have children who never see a diploma.

Cycles!

How do we break them?

It wasn't too surprising to discover that the vast majority of prisoners in our country are high school dropouts. Many of them don't know how to read or to write. Their parents didn't know how to read or write, either.

One time I played the role of Clarence Darrow in the one-man play made famous by Henry Fonda. Darrow, the famed agnostic attorney, was probably best known as the lawyer who defended John Scopes in the infamous "Monkey Trial." Although an agnostic, Darrow had some keen insight into humanity. He said, "History repeats itself. That's one of the things that's wrong with history."

He was talking about world history, but I think it's true for family history as well.

As I stand in the hall on duty, clearly visible in my suit, I watch the students and I listen. I'm often appalled at their language. Their conversations are filled with the "f" word. If you tell them to watch their language they look at you like you're from the Dark Ages.

I shudder, too, at the way many dress and the hairstyles they wear. It looks like they've watched too many rock videos. One day here comes a kid, Bart, toward my classroom in a T-Shirt that reads: "S— Happens." I stop him and tell him he can't wear it into class. "I have First Amendment rights!" he says, as he yanks off his earphones that are connected to his portable compact disc player. The CD is spinning the newest disc of his favorite heavy metal band, "Faith No More."

"You're not wearing that shirt in my classroom," I say gently but firmly. "I don't think you should wear it to school." The truth is, I wonder how his parents could allow him to even own such a shirt let alone wear it to school, but then I wonder to what degree his parents are involved in his life.

"I can take you to court!" he shouts in defiance.

"Then I'll see you there," I answer gently.

"You're a prude, man! Get a life!" he says as he storms away.

My heart aches. I know that it is circumstances like this that have caused many Christians to leave public schools in favor of Christian schools and home schooling. Many also fear a curriculum that promotes secular humanistic values. Others object to public schools that promote "safe sex" rather than abstinence, and teach homosexuality as an "acceptable lifestyle." We read of New York City schools openly distributing condoms and agree that the message it promotes is not chastity, nor is it the sanctity of marriage. In the society that calls Magic Johnson and Pee Wee

Herman heroes, it would be easy to throw up our hands, say we've lost, isolate ourselves, and pretend to live in a vacuum, but as Bart goes to his locker to change his shirt, I've never felt more strongly that this is not the time to wave the white flag of surrender.

I respect the parents who have decided to educate their children outside the public schools and I understand their reasons. If I felt that my children were being harmed or that their faith was being ridiculed in a public school, I would seek alternate schooling for them as well. Parents must ultimately decide what is best for their children.

But the vast majority of students in America still attend public schools. The vast majority have no other option. We have an inherent responsibility as a society to make public schools institutions of which we can be proud. If we are unhappy with them, we have no one to blame but ourselves as they are merely products of the society we have created.

Likewise, if we wish to have the schools improved, we must look to ourselves. Every decision that affects public schools is a political decision. Yet many of the Christians who complain have never attended a school board meeting or called a school board member. Many do not even know who their school board members are. School board elections generally receive the poorest voter turnout of any elections held, and yet these members are formulating policy and adopting curriculum which will influence our children and our society for hundreds of years to come.

Cycles!

Don't look for someone else to do something. Ever since I started teaching in 1975, I've been saying that if parents would take the responsibility which is theirs, we wouldn't have nine out of the ten problems we have in the schools of America. So go do something about it!

(There, now I've gotten it off my chest and I'm climbing down from my soapbox.)

Now let's look again at the family and the gifts it gives. When I look at students like Bart ("Get a life, man!"), I don't need a degree in sociology to see whether or not they've received the gift of self-worth, nor do I need a degree in psychology to know whether or not they've received the next gift we're going to discuss, *the gift of stability.*

Foundations must be stable. Jesus tells a parable that contrasts a wise and a foolish builder:

> Therefore everyone who hears these words of mine and puts them into practice is like a wise man who built his house on the rock. The rain came down, the streams rose, and the winds blew and beat against the house; yet it did not fall, because it had its foundation on the rock. But everyone who hears these words of mine and does not put them into practice is like a foolish man who built his house on the sand. The rain came down, the streams rose, and the winds blew and beat against that house, and it fell with a great crash.
>
> (Matt. 7: 24-27)

I trace the bulk of the problems with kids, in fact, the bulk of the problems in America, to the fact that we haven't been building our homes on the "Rock."

Ethics and morality in society, truth in government, corporate greed—it all goes back to the foundation on which we chose to build our lives, doesn't it? And for the most part, we build that foundation during childhood.

What frightens me is that the effects of sin are cumulative. I read that people picketed *Gone With the Wind* when it first appeared in 1939 because Rhett Butler told Scarlett he didn't "give a damn." To most people today that is almost humorous, but it illustrates just how used to profanity saints have become.

Gone With the Wind would receive a "G" rating today and our children, accustomed to the profanity of rap music and R-rated movies, could never believe that at one time Christians picketed *Gone With the Wind* for its use of a swear word.

Let's zero in on the stability of the foundations we are laying. The stability is established in the home.

Each year more and more graduating students come from single parent families. As we all know, divorce has reached epidemic proportions. There are whole books and thousands of studies on the effects of divorce on children, and I'm certainly not an expert. In some cases I'm sure that divorce may actually make for a *more* stable environment for a child, but it is my opinion, based on simple observation, this is usually not the case.

Once again I'm outside on hall duty and I'm "clearly visible." The students are obviously more excited about coming to class today than they were yesterday. I know it's because this is Friday and it's also the last hour of the day. One more hour and then a break from school, if only for the weekend. I greet each of them, usually by name, as they come into my classroom. Although I shudder at the behavior of some of them there are those who make it all worthwhile. Then I remember that even the ones who could take the joy out of teaching are special gifts of God. I've discovered that obnoxious qualities in students are really cries for help and attention.

On this particular day I greet three guys as they enter my room. They look like "Hi, I'm Larry and this is my brother Darryl, and this is my other brother Darryl," from television fame. But they are friendly and greet me warmly asking, "Got any big plans for the weekend, Mr. Doud?" I tell them no.

Here come two girls in their blue and white cheerleading uniforms. There's a game tonight. They don't walk into my room, they bounce. As soon as they are seated, they open their purses and take out their make-up cases. They don't even acknowledge my greeting, they're so busy talking and so unaware of the rest of the world about them.

Clarance is next. His cowboy boots are about two steps ahead of the rest of his body. He has a belt buckle the size of a small shield on his belt. I can see the outline of a tobacco can in his back pocket. I check his mouth for lumps to see if he has remembered to get rid of his "chew." There are no noticeable lumps. I greet him. He grunts in acknowledgment. I don't think he's real excited about studying split infinitives.

The next young man in a bright red sweater is the best student in the class. He agonizes over any mistakes he makes on a test and will argue with me about answers. He expects perfection of himself, and he'd never guess that he intimidates me because it's obvious he's much brighter than I am. His parents are professional people. He sits right at the front of the classroom and would answer every question if I would let him. Before I have a chance, he greets me first and comments on how much he enjoyed his homework.

And here comes Shon. I wonder if he'll talk today. Usually when I say, "Hi," he simply nods his head. He sits all by himself in class. He never talks to anyone else and no one talks to him except once when one of the cheerleaders asked him if he wanted to buy a homecoming button. His face turned completely red but he opened his wallet and handed her a dollar. She said, "Thanks." I've watched him in the lunchroom and he sits alone there, too. There's always a distant look in his eyes. When I talk to him in class, he answers but he never looks me in the eye.

"What are you going to do this weekend, Shon?" I ask him, deciding not to say, "Hi."

"I'm going to see my mom."

His answer takes me aback. I know nothing about his family. "You get to see your mom very often?" I ask.

And then he looks me right in the eye, as if there were still some hope—that I have an explanation. "I haven't seen her in nine years," he says. "She deserted us." Then he walks past me into the classroom and takes his seat. I'm about to follow him, feeling the need to say something more when I'm stopped by another teacher. Later, just before starting the lesson on split infinitives, I tell Shon I'll be thinking about him during the weekend, hoping that all will go well between him and his mother. He doesn't answer except to give the customary shake of his head.

I begin: "Infinitives, class. One type of verbal. What are the other two types of verbals again?" And the bright boy in the bright red sweater immediately raises his hand, but I look over his head at Shon, who is looking down at his desk.

I'm sure Shon would be surprised to learn that not only did I think about him that weekend in 1985, but I've been thinking about him ever since.

I understand why Shon didn't seem too excited about the lesson on split infinitives. I, too, didn't get too excited about learning when I was in grade school. In fact, I forgot most of what happened to me during those years, including what I should have learned, because my mind wasn't really there. It was on what was going on at home.

I don't how many times Dad left home. Sometimes he would only be gone for two or three days and sometimes he'd be gone for weeks. The time he was gone the longest was the time we had to get the door fixed. I don't know what he and Mother were arguing about. I went into the room I shared with my brother and sisters and shut the door and put my hands over my ears. I just wanted it to stop. Like Mom, I just wanted everything in our family to be happy. Even though I had my hands over my ears and I think I was crying, I could still hear their shouting.

Terrified, I ran from my room into the kitchen. There my mother sat at the kitchen table in her usual spot, crying hysterically. Dad was gone again. He slammed the door as he left. I tried to comfort Mom, but I felt in need of comfort myself. Why couldn't our family get along? Why did I have to worry about whether or not I was going to continue to have a family?

After several days I would ask: "Mom, when is Dad coming home?"

"I don't know, Dear," she would answer gently.

And after a few more days I would ask again, "Mom, when is Dad coming home?"

And again she would reply, "I don't know, Dear."

And after a week I must have sounded a bit more burdened when I asked, "Mom, is Dad coming home pretty soon?"

She shot back, "I don't know!" And then a moment later said, "Come here, Dear." She held me and we cried together.

I tried hard to forget about that stuff, but I can't because this is the stuff of which my foundation was made. I'm in the process of building a new foundation for myself so that my children never have to experience what I did. The best way to get rid of the faulty foundation is to bring all the stuff out of the closet and take it to the dump. And that's what I am doing, a little at a time, and it feels so very good.

The gift of stability is one of the greatest gifts a family can give a child. Stability means knowing that home is there, that it's a safe place with a mom and dad who are devoted to their children's welfare. If parents are divorced they can still create a stable environment for their children, but it can never be the same as a home where a mother and father both live under the same roof and dedicate themselves to fostering their children's self-worth.

◆

The gift of stability is one of the greatest gifts a family can give a child. Stability means knowing that home is there, that it's a safe place with a mom and dad who are devoted to their children's welfare.

◆

I recognize that there are others besides the parents involved in helping create a stable environment for a child, but the brunt of the responsibility really rests with our biological parents, doesn't it?

Tammy and I have read our children the familiar story of "The Three Little Pigs" many times. I'm sure you, too, know the story well. It's really a story about foundations, isn't it? It's very similar to the parable Jesus told in Matthew 7 about the wise and foolish builders. The wise man built his house upon a rock, a strong foundation. It stood in the times of storm. One of the three pigs' house was strong and secure—established upon a strong foundation. When the wolf came he could not destroy the house. How do we fight off the big, bad wolf whose name is Satan? How do we fend off the evil one who seeks to destroy our homes? We must have homes built on stable foundations. Children must be given this gift of a secure foundation or they are likely to forever feel insecure.

Cycles!

I must have been asking myself, "Is Dad coming home?" when I should have been thinking about math. Dad always came home, but I never felt secure. Dad came home and nothing was said. It was like he'd never been gone. He and Mother went back to the usual routine and he took his place again in front of the television. Had I imagined it had happened? My parents never divorced but that doesn't mean ours was a stable home. I'm sure many children from divorced homes enjoyed more stability than I experienced. I was forever worried and anxious that I wasn't going to have a family. Part of me still is.

Oh, for homes built upon the "Rock!" Solid. Secure. Stable. The gift of stability is one of the greatest gifts a family can give. It is a gift that helps us discover our sainthood and live like "saints in the light."

I burped. It was a big, big burp that came from deep within. Seth, our oldest, looked at me and asked: "Dad, what are you supposed to say?"

"I don't know, what am I supposed to say?" I answered.

"You are supposed to say 'excuse me,'" Seth said, enjoying instructing me.

"You're excused," I said as soon as he finished saying, "Excuse me."

"No!" Seth screamed. "**You** are supposed to say 'excuse me.'"

"You're excused," I said again.

"No! **You're** supposed to say it." Seth was indignant.

"Say what?" I asked.

"Excuse me." Seth answered again.

"You're excused," I said as sincerely as I could.

"Dad!" Seth was totally frustrated now. "Say it, Dad!"

"What?" I asked innocently.

"You know what!" Seth was smiling even though he was trying

to seem angry.

"No, I don't," said innocent me. "What are you talking about?" Innocent me.

"You burped real loud, Dad, and you didn't say, 'excuse me,'" Seth said.

"You're excused," I said and then shielded myself as Seth playfully started beating up on me.

I was only able to do this routine with Seth a few times before he caught on, and then I had to pull it on unsuspecting Luke, our next oldest. He doesn't fall for it any more, either. Jessica, the next in line, is a prime candidate now and I'm just waiting for the right opportunity to do it to her. I won't be able to use Zachary as a victim for a couple of years yet.

Now, if I burp and Seth hears me, he simply says "Set a good example, Dad."

My dad would not only burp, but he would, you guessed it, burp as loudly as he could. Then he'd laugh about it. The louder he'd do it the better. I remember the first time I looked at him and asked as I pinched my nose, "What are you supposed to say, Dad?"

He answered: "I don't know. What am I supposed to say?"

"You're supposed to say, 'excuse me.'" I enjoyed instructing him.

"You're excused," he'd answer as soon as I said, "Excuse me."

"No!" I shrieked. "**You** are supposed to say, 'Excuse me.'"

And you guessed it, he'd answer, "You're excused." He did the same thing to me I now do to my kids. I loved it, just as mine do. Unlike Seth, however, I never told my dad that he should set a good example. I guess I didn't know he wasn't setting a good example.

Example. One of the most important gifts a family gives. It

comprises a great big part of the foundation you take with you from childhood.

Most of us will discipline our children the way our parents disciplined us. I remember visiting with a man who was prohibited from seeing his son because he had habitually beaten him with a belt. "My dad use to beat me 'til I couldn't walk," he said, "and it didn't do me any harm."

Some of us open our packages on Christmas Eve. Some on Christmas morning. Some open a few on Christmas Eve and the rest of them on Christmas morning. Usually the determining factor is how we did it when we were kids.

◆

Many of us never discover our sainthood because we've never really known a saint. There has been no one there to set the example.

◆

When I sneeze, I'll finish my "hutchoo" by adding "choo-chootrain." That's the way my dad did it.

These examples from childhood—they are habits of the heart. Some are good, and some can produce devastating effects that are passed on from generation to generation.

Basically, the point is this: Many of us never discover our sainthood because we've never really known a saint. There has been no one there to set the example. We may come in contact with saints from outside our families who will have a powerful influence on us, but it's not the same as being raised by a mother and father who are conscious of their sainthood and are themselves a child's best example.

Let me ask you, are you the type of Christian that you want your children to become?

Oh, I know, none of us is perfect and certainly there are no perfect families. There is no family that can give all the gifts to a child that he or she needs. But that doesn't let us off the hook. Parents are the greatest teachers in their children's lives. Period. And their most powerful method of teaching is example. Children learn what they see.

Many of the things learned from the family may seem really trivial—like how to answer the phone. But some other lessons learned through the examples set for us in our families become main factors in determining our futures.

◆

The gift of example is one of the most important gifts a family gives.

◆

Last year I went to see one of our school counselors about a student who told me she was going to drop out of school. He said, "Oh, well, she's a—," and he named her last name and explained she was one of a large family of children, none of whom had ever graduated from high school.

Is it surprising that children who come from alcoholic homes are much more likely to become alcoholics themselves? Or that children who are the victims of physical or sexual abuse are more likely to become abusers? Or that children whose parents were rageaholics are much more likely to rage at their own children? And on and on.

But think of all the implications here. How important is the example set for children? How awesome is the responsibility of parenthood!

We must recognize that who we are, right now, has been largely determined through examples modeled to us by our parents. We must keep those characteristics and habits that are good and healthy and discard those that are harmful. If we don't know, we truly may not see the difference, God is able to help us distinguish between that which is good and that which is harmful. The Holy Spirit will open our eyes to the way we should be living and the example that we should be setting, not only for our families but for other saints on their journeys. It is difficult, however, to know *how* to turn to the Holy Spirit and allow Him to minister to us if we've never had someone set an example for us. This is where the larger family of believers plays such an important role, but we'll discuss that later.

The gift of example is one of the most important gifts a family gives. It may determine how often you bathe or brush your teeth or whether you graduate from high school or college or graduate school. It may also determine whether or not you receive the greatest gift of all—the gift of faith, which we'll discuss in the next chapter.

We all graduate from childhood with a foundation of some kind. The foundation is comprised of hundreds of habits—the way we go about doing things we have learned. We learn most of these habits from those who have been our most important examples, our parents.

I can just picture Seth, Luke, Jessica, Zachary someday. They'll burp in front of their kids and they'll hear, "What are you supposed to say?"

And each of them will answer innocently, "I don't know. What am I supposed to say?"

"You're supposed to say, 'excuse me'," our grandchildren will instruct them.

And one of our four kids will say, "You're excused," and the whole cycle will turn again.

I will have taught them that.

The Gift of Faith

*W*e're supposed to get six inches of snow today. Everyone is complaining, except me. I love the snow. It makes everything look so clean. As I look out my window toward Lake Superior I can see that it has already begun. Funny, it's snowing sideways. How does it do that?

Several years ago I was traveling, and when I arrived at my hotel room I turned on the television. It had already been tuned to a station that played rock music videos. One glance and I was sickened by what I saw. The caption informed me that the title of the album was "Living in Sin" and the name of the group was Bon Jovi. I started to switch the channel but remembered that this group and its lead singer, Jon Bon Jovi, was the favorite of one of the students on my high school debate team. So I decided I would watch.

As one of the band members jumped across the stage, the camera panned the audience at a concert. The audience was mostly young kids. They were screaming and raising their hands in the air as though in worship to the god of rock, and they were pressing toward the front of the stage straining to touch members of the band as though they sought healing.

A girl near the front held high a sign that read "JON! I WILL DIE FOR YOU!" I stared at the sign. I looked again at the face of the girl. I believe she meant it.

That was several years ago. I have since seen rock videos that imitate explicit sex and contain graphic violence and nudity. The average teenager in America spends about three hours a day watching television, and much of that time is spent watching rock videos. Some of the rock videos make no pretense—they glorify Satan, are filled with Satanic images, and they outwardly mock Christ.

◆

Who is going to be the one to tell the kids that a Christian is one whose life is a sign held up for everyone to read? And the sign reads, "Jesus! I will live for you!" Who will tell them that?

◆

I am angry and I am pessimistic. Oh, rock videos are not the problem. They are only one symptom of a society that continues to morally deteriorate. It's not getting better. Oh, yes, I have met hundreds of fine young men and women who want their lives to count for Jesus Christ and are set on following Him. But, at the same time, the facts speak for themselves. Our young people are in crisis. Despite all the attempts to teach "safe sex," the number of sexually transmitted diseases is skyrocketing, as is the adolescent pregnancy rate. Chemical abuse and suicide are on the rise, too. What is the future going to be like for my children and my children's children?

I am angry. Who is going to be the one to tell the kids that a Christian is one whose life is a sign held up for everyone to read? And the sign reads, "JESUS! I WILL LIVE FOR YOU!" Who will tell them that?

It's snowing more heavily now.

Don't get me wrong, I haven't given up on kids. I'm not angry at them. Kids don't make the movies or produce pornography. Adults do! They're not the ones importing cocaine. Adults are! It's obvious that of all the gifts parents give their children the least likely to be passed on to them is the example of a committed, Christian faith that works. Yet it is *this* gift that is needed if we are ever going to discover our sainthood and enjoy the abundant life.

Parents are pretty good about passing on their denominational affiliations. If they are Lutherans, their children usually become Lutherans. If they are Presbyterians, their children usually become Presbyterians. And Catholic parents usually have Catholic children and Baptist parents, Baptist children, and Nazarene parents, Nazarene children, and so on and so on and so on.

Cycles!

But what about genuine faith? It must be modeled in the home. It must be one of the most precious gifts parents give their children. I know that parents can't believe for their children or have faith for them. Children must develop a faith of their own, but chances are that most of the time whatever faith a child develops is going to be like Mom's or Dad's.

Scripture tells parents to "Train a child in the way he should go, and when he is old he will not turn from it" (Prov. 22:6). That training is the foundation on which a saint builds a life, and the training must include the example of a mature Christian faith. It is the only way to experience the abundant life.

Jesus tells us, "I have come that they may have life, and have it to the full" (John 10:10). The Gospel of John mentions the word *life* 36 times. That's twice as many times as any other New Testament book. "Life, abundant life" is a great theme of the gospel of John.

John records these words, "My sheep listen to my voice; I know them, and they follow me. I give them eternal life, and they shall never perish; no one can snatch them out of my hand" (John 10:27-28).

What a promise!

It is also John who records this great statement of Christ's: "I am the way and the truth and the life. No one comes to the Father except through me" (John 14:6).

Several things are evident from these verses:

1. It is Christ who gives us life eternal. Life is a gift from Him.
2. Christ, in fact, is life. He is everything life really is.
3. He is our example, and we like sheep are to follow Him.
4. Abundant life—life to the full—can only be known when we follow the example of Jesus Christ.

This is our faith. It is abundant life found in Jesus Christ. We need to share it with a society whose doctors now consider depression the number one health problem. Take a look around you. Are the people you know really experiencing the fullness of abundant life in Christ? What about those people with whom you work each day? Or the ones who work in that restaurant where you like to eat? Or what about your favorite movie stars? How many people do you know who really live a committed Christian life?

Although we must share this faith with adults, the foundation of faith should begin in childhood. Christian parents should be the ones who model this abundant life—this faith—for their children. Many children come to a saving faith outside the home, but again, for most, home is really where the heart is and it provides the greatest example.

One of the spiritual mentors in my life has a saying that may or may not be original with him. I've thought about it a lot. It goes,

◆

Children must develop a faith of their own, but chances are that most of the time whatever faith a child develops is going to be like Mom's or Dad's.

◆

"The greatest distance in the world is the distance between the head and the heart." I believe it.

The greatest barrier keeping many of us from living a truly abundant Christian life is that we have a head faith and not a heart faith. We acknowledge Christ with our minds but we save our hearts for all the things we really desire—which are often the same things our parents desired. We want nice cars, nice homes, nice jobs, nice friends, nice vacations, nice clothes, nice kids, nice lives, and we pour all of our energy into trying to gain the things we desire. We forget the simple truth that "where your treasure is, there your heart will be also" (Matt. 6:21).

Head faith fails to satisfy our basic need of love because love is a need of the heart. True faith is a heart faith. Scripture tells us plainly: "For it is with your heart that you believe" (Rom. 10:10).

The heart is also where God looks: "The Lord does not look at the things man looks at. Man looks at the outward appearance, but the Lord looks at the heart" (1 Sam. 16:7).

And the heart is where children look, too.

Mom and Dad may say they believe and that Christ is important to them, but the habits of the heart will reveal how real that faith is.

Years ago when I first moved to the Brainerd area, I heard about a split in one of the local congregations. The split occurred because the pastor had announced to his congregation that he would not be conducting confirmation classes any longer. He told the parents that if their children desired to be confirmed, they would need to approach him individually and confess their faith and desire to become members of the church. I later learned that this pastor had become frustrated with the confirmation process in his church. He believed that young people of confirmation age were being confirmed simply because it was expected of them and not because they really wanted to believe. He had witnessed how after confirmation many of the young people dropped out of the church or failed to become active in it. He said he was tired of confirming people who would simply believe with their heads rather than their hearts.

Well, a split in the church occurred because there were those in the congregation who supported the pastor, and there were those who wanted to see him fired. One irate church member said,"My son will never take the initiative to come see you or confess his faith!"

"Then he doesn't really want to join the body of Christ, does he?" was the pastor's response.

Paul warns Timothy,
There will be terrible times in the last days. People will be lovers of themselves, lovers of money, boastful,

proud, abusive, disobedient to their parents, ungrateful, unholy, without love, unforgiving, slanderous, without self-control, brutal, not lovers of the good, treacherous, rash, conceited, lovers of pleasure rather than lovers of God—having a form of godliness but denying its power. Have nothing to do with them.

(2 Tim. 3: 1-5)

Sound familiar? You see, head faith is but "a form of godliness" and can't substitute for a committed heart. Oh, for parents whose hearts are committed to the Lord Jesus and model that commitment to their children!

Another barrier that keeps many of us from the abundant life of heartfelt faith is that we think of God's love in human terms. Most children will never know any greater love on earth than that given them by their parents. Even so, parental love is imperfect. But since this love from parents is usually the main source of love in a child's life, he will tend to equate God's love with parental love. Consequently, many of us grow up with a distorted picture of what the love of God is truly like. We tend to see God's love coming with strings attached. Or we see it as being quickly withdrawn if we fail to perform up to required expectations. Some of us grow up believing that God has favorites and He doesn't really love me as much as He loves my older sister.

Over the years, as I've counseled people, I couldn't begin to guess how many have said they picture God, their Heavenly Father, in the same way they picture their earthly fathers. For many, that man was detached and uninvolved in their lives. For others, the man they picture is a harsh parent who watches every move and is just waiting to "get out the belt" should they step out of line.

Victims whose parents physically or sexually abused them have a particularly difficult time conceiving of a loving, tender, compassionate heavenly parent.

As a child, I would obey my father because I feared him. Fear was the basic motivation. It's not surprising, then, that my obedience to God began with fear as well. If I didn't measure up, God would send to me hell where the flames would dance fueled by my soul. Fear is a worthy motivator, but it can't compare to love. God's name is LOVE—not fear.

Read these following verses over and over again. Study them. Memorize them. I've read them for years but am only now truly coming to appreciate their full meaning:

> If anyone acknowledges that Jesus is the Son of God, God lives in him and he in God. And so we know and rely on the love God has for us. God is love, Whoever lives in love lives in God, and God in him. Love is made complete among us so that we will have confidence on the day of judgment, because in this world we are like him. There is no fear in love. But perfect love drives out fear, because fear has to do with punishment. The one who fears is not made perfect in love. We love because he first loved us.
>
> (1 John 4:15-19)

"We love because he first loved us." That's why we love God — not because if we don't He's going to hunt us down and shoot us. We love Him because He first loved us. When we have the faith to believe how complete God's love for us is, the head and the heart become one.

Faith is available to all of us. God has no favorites. Christ tells us that He stands at the door of our hearts asking entrance. He says, "Here I am! I stand at the door and knock. If anyone hears my voice and opens the door, I will come in and eat with him, and he with me" (Rev. 3:20).

All we have to do is open the door to our hearts. The grace of Jesus Christ does the rest. We need not fear.

For it is by grace you have been saved, through faith—and this not from yourselves, it is the gift of God—not by works, so that no one can boast. For we are God's workmanship, created in Christ Jesus to do good works, which God prepared in advance for us to do (Eph. 2: 8-10).

It's God's grace through faith that does the saving. Grace. Amazing grace! Another one of my spiritual mentors, says, "Grace is the face God wears when He meets us in our sin."

God intends for mothers and fathers to teach their children through example of a faith not only of the head, but also of the heart. If parents model this type of faith, most children will grow up with an entirely different attitude of who God is. They'll know a God whom they will welcome into their hearts. Of course, a child may choose to rebel no matter how good the parental example. In that case, parents must give their children another gift God gives us, the gift of freedom. We talk about that in the next chapter. I believe that most of the time, if children see genuine faith modeled in the lives of their parents, they are going to want that faith, too.

In the process of writing this book, I shared with some friends what I believe to be some of the gifts a family gives—the same things I've been sharing with you. The following week, one of these friends approached me, her eyes filled with tears.

"I've been a terrible parent," she said. "Neither my husband nor

I gave our children the gifts of which you spoke. I think our kids grew up believing that all that mattered to us was drinking. Now they've all moved away from home. I look at them and see their messed-up lives. I have a son who is an alcoholic, just like his dad. My daughter's been married and divorced twice and is trying to raise three children on her own. I see her doing to her kids the same things I did to her. I feel guilty. I feel so very guilty, but I never received any of those gifts from my parents either."

Cycles!

I handed her the box of tissue from my desk and let her know I had heard her and recognized her pain. Then I said, "We need to go home and learn all over again."

"My children would never all move home again, and my parents are dead." She hadn't understood what I said.

"No. Your children can't come home and you can't go home, but you can come to Christ as a child with a childlike faith that simply wants to believe. The Bible says that we can, in fact, we must 'be born again.' That doesn't happen until we come to Jesus as little children and let Him teach us how to live."

"Oh, I was born again when I was only eight," she said, "but I've been a backslider most of my life."

"I hear you saying that you've never really experienced much of the abundance that Christ promised," I said gently.

"Abundance?" She almost laughed. "Life has been one series of problems. Good things happen to other people. Not to me."

"Christ is able to give you an abundant life. Christ is able to give your children abundant life. Do you believe that?" I asked.

"I don't know any more. I just feel so guilty about how I raised my kids." The guilt screamed from her face.

I prayed with her there in my office. I told her that God loved her despite her doubts. Together we claimed the promises of forgiveness together that John also writes about, "If we confess our sins, he is faithful and just and will forgive us our sins and purify us from all unrighteousness" (1 John 1:9).

I especially get excited about the verse that says God not only forgives our sins but He also forgets that we ever committed them (Jer. 31:34), removing them from us "as far as the east is from the west," (Ps. 103:12).

And this verse excites me, too: "'Come now, let us reason together,' says the Lord. 'Though your sins are like scarlet, they shall be as white as snow; though they are red as crimson, they shall be like wool'" (Isa. 1:18).

I'm looking out at Superior again. It has stopped snowing. We didn't get even close to six inches. The fresh, new blanket of snow looks so white and clean—just like a forgiven heart.

The Gift of Freedom

Beth and Luke each got a pair of Rollerblades for Christmas. That's one of the things they really wanted—one of many things they "really" wanted. The trouble is, it's difficult to use Rollerblades during the winter in Minnesota. Roads and sidewalks are usually ice coated, and besides, it's too cold outside. They'd freeze their noses off. So, they've been begging to go to the roller skating rink where they can "break in their blades."

Well, they've gone several times already in the three weeks since Christmas. But you know kids, they would like to go every day.

They'd like to skip school and go Rollerblading.

They'd like to skip eating and go Rollerblading.

They'd like to skip sleeping and go Rollerblading.

They'd Rollerblade their lives away if you'd let them.

I'm amazed at them as they zip around the rink. Wasn't it just yesterday they were in diapers?

Tammy and I are in agreement about when we are going to let them start dating. We think they'll be ready when they reach the age of 21. We'll let them start then, as long as one of us goes along to chaperone.

Jessica, our four-year-old, rents skates at the rink—she's not into Rollerblades—yet. When I finished tying her skates the other day, she took off like she knew what she was doing, but she didn't. She fell. I helped her up. She took off again. She fell again. I helped her up again. She took off more cautiously then, but soon down she went. I held her hand and walked her around, pulling her up each time she began to fall. After a few minutes of my help she said, "I can do it on my own, Dad." So I let her go. She took a few steps and down she went.

Jessica has already told us she wants her training wheels taken off her bike next summer. I wonder if she is really ready for that. What do you think? At what age should the training wheels come off? Sure would hate to have her get hurt.

◆

Freedom is another of the essential foundational gifts a family gives. It is the gift that allows a child to grow and become a unique individual.

◆

There are no skates or bikes in Zachary's life yet. He just turned two. He is our last one in diapers. He drives his "motorcycle" around the house, crashing into things and falling on the floor pretending he's dead. His tongue hangs out of his mouth and everything. Quite the actor. He goes grocery shopping with Tammy and shoots all the other shoppers with his imaginary gun. Tammy is trying to break him of this habit and says that he's getting better. The last time they went shopping he only shot two people.

I called home last night, and Zachary put up quite a fuss with his mother because he wanted to talk to me. He never has anything to say, though, except, "Hi. Hi. Hi. Hi." But last night he carried on a regular conversation. I couldn't recognize any of his words, but you could tell from his intonation that it all made sense to him. I'm afraid he might have been telling me that he wants a pair of Rollerblades, too.

Yes, Rollerblades were one of the things Seth and Luke really wanted. But all too soon they will outgrow them and will need bigger ones. That will mean buying them another gift. Maybe by then they'll have their own money and can buy their own skates. I can wish.

Rollerblades will be only one of the many hundreds of gifts Tammy and I will give our children. I'm sure if we figure it out we'll spend a small fortune on gifts for them over the years. Don't scold us, though. If you have kids you're doing the same thing.

But how many of us parents realize that the most important gifts we give our children have nothing to do with money? Think about it. What was the most important gift your parents ever gave you? Did they give you the gifts of self-worth, stability, example, and faith that we've been discussing? These are the most important gifts and they can't be bought in a store.

What about the gift of freedom? Freedom is another of the essential foundational gifts a family gives. It is the gift that allows a child to grow and become a unique individual. It is the gift that allows him to make choices, even incorrect ones, and experience the consequences of those choices. The gift of freedom is the gift of letting go. The challenge for parents is knowing how to give their children the appropriate amount of freedom at the right time.

We haven't taken Jessica's training wheels off yet, but come next summer, they're history. We'll save them, though, for

Zachary's first bike.

This is all very obvious, so obvious that we often take it for granted. I've discovered that one of the greatest sources of discontent in people's lives is that they do not know how to set appropriate boundaries. They often are miserable because their boundaries are either too legalistic and binding, or don't exist at all. One of the greatest gifts a family and parents can give is the gift of teaching their children how to enjoy life and yet know how to exercise self-discipline.

I have seen teenagers whose parents have not given them any freedom. They are usually not very healthy kids. On the other hand, I've known too many young people whose parents have given them almost total freedom since they were very young. Basically, the message these kids have received is that their parents are disinterested in their lives, and so they seek love elsewhere.

There must be a healthy balance of freedom and restraint. Parents must seek God's wisdom in knowing how to allow their children to make their own decisions at appropriate times in their lives.

Our kids are still at the age where they think they want to live with Mom and Dad for the rest of their lives. There is no need right now to tell them someday they'll have to be out on their own. They'll come to that realization soon enough. I remember when I first realized I wasn't going to be able to live at home all my life and that my mother couldn't be my wife. It was a frightening thought. It was followed by thinking that maybe I could buy the house next door and live there when I "grew up."

Our kids would just as soon be in the company of their parents as they would the company of their friends, but I know that will change. Our two oldest boys are already a little embarrassed when we hug them in front of their friends.

I remember that I was embarrassed, too, when my mother

would drive me to high school. She'd say: "Give your mother a kiss, Dear." The day I protested that my friends made fun of me, she said, "You should never be ashamed to give your mother a kiss. You are never too big to kiss your mother. Don't you know how much I love you? Don't you love me?"

I felt such guilt. Of course, I knew she loved me, but did I have to kiss her to show my love to her? Because I felt so much guilt about her lack of love from my father, I kissed her good bye.

◆

True love cannot be demanded or commanded or forced or manipulated by fear, guilt, or shame. Love must be the product of free will just as patriotism is the product of a free society.

◆

Just as perfect love casts out fear, it also casts out guilt. Parents who use guilt and shame to motivate their children are not giving them the gift of freedom. True love cannot be demanded or commanded or forced or manipulated by fear, guilt, or shame. Love must be the product of free will just as patriotism is the product of a free society.

My mother had no idea that she failed to give me the gift of freedom. She would never have consciously done anything to hurt her children. And yet today, fifteen years since her death, I'm still struggling to accept the fact I'm not being judged on whether or not I jump through all the right hoops.

Our best model of this gift of freedom is God, Himself. This is the gift He gives us. We are free to love Him or to reject Him. We are free to serve Him or serve ourselves. Of course as with any of our decisions there are consequences that result because of our choices.

God started out by giving man quite a liberal boundary. God said, "You are free to eat from any tree in the garden" (Gen. 2:16). It is clear that God intended for man and woman to live forever. There would be no cancer, no heart disease, no sexually transmitted diseases, no crippling arthritis, and no Alzheimer's disease. Man and woman walked the Garden of Eden naked, yet knew no shame.

God established only one boundary. He said to Adam and Eve, "You must not eat from the tree of the knowledge of good and evil" (Gen. 2:17).

Why did God establish this boundary? Basically what God was saying to Adam and Eve is, "Don't try to be God. Let me be God." The serpent tells Eve, "'You will not surely die...for God knows that when you eat of it your eyes will be opened, and you will be like God, knowing good and evil" (Gen. 3:4, 5).

Adam and Eve did the one thing God asked them not to do. They ate from the tree, and death entered the world. God had told them what the consequence would be, "When you eat of it [the tree of the knowledge of good and evil] you will surely die" (Gen. 2:17).

I don't know how many times I've been asked the question: "Why, if God loves us, did He allow Adam and Eve to eat of that tree? Why does He allow suffering? Why didn't He put a big tall fence around the tree? Why did He put the tree in the Garden to begin with?"

God allowed Adam and Eve to freely eat of the tree for the same reason we'll take the training wheels off Jessica's bike next summer. God allowed Adam and Eve to freely eat of the tree for the same reason we'll someday allow our children to date. If we love our children, we have to give them their freedom. God loves us, His children, and so He has given us our freedom. Love cannot exist without freedom. If God had made us incapable of making bad choices, He would have made us robots. Robots are incapable of love.

As a parent, I must admit there are times I wish my children were robots and all I had to do was program them by pushing the right buttons. Then they would perform exactly as I want them to. Robots don't cause you any pain or get hurt feelings or demand your attention, but neither do robots sit on your lap and give you kisses on your cheeks and tell you that, "You're the best daddy in the whole world." No, despite all the pain being human can bring, *I'll experience the depths of despair if only to know the fullness of love.*

Saints are those who live in the fullness of love because they have experienced the gift of freedom. It is one of the most cherished gifts parents can give their children. It is one of God's most cherished gifts to us.

You know, I think I might just buy myself a pair of Rollerblades. It looks like a lot of fun.

The Journey

Starting Over / Letting Go

etty started making really weird sounds just outside Motley. I ignored them. She had been such a faithful car during my two years at Brainerd State Junior College and had made the sixty-mile round trip from my home in Staples to Brainerd hundreds of times. I loved Betty. She was entitled to make a few weird sounds.

I hoped whatever was wrong would just go away. If I ignored the problem, I didn't have to acknowledge it. If I didn't acknowledge it, it didn't exist. Great reasoning, huh?

A lot of good that line of thinking did me when Betty's brakes failed coming into Staples. Thankfully, I was able to coast to a stop on the highway, by rubbing the tire on the front passenger's side along the curb.

The mechanic told me more than I wanted to hear. "This car is ready for the junk pile, I'm afraid. Cost too much to get it fixed up so it'll be safe to drive."

But this was *Betty,* Grandpa Guy's car. He always kept her shined and polished and I helped him. This car was a thousand memories. I would not accept the fact that Betty's days were over.

"Yeah, you're going to need a new car." The mechanic was a complete stoic. He had just told me that one of my best friends had died and he didn't even care.

I wished that I were more stoical. I had read where a man named Walpole had said that, "The world is a comedy for those who think, a tragedy for those who feel." I definitely am a feeler—an extreme feeler. I cry hysterically over sentimental television commercials. (It is hard to be like this in a society where it isn't very acceptable for men to be too emotional.)

I didn't cry in front of the mechanic, but I did when I got home and told Mom about it. I cried and Mom cried, too.

I didn't have the heart to get rid of Betty, so I brought her home and left her sitting in the backyard. Sometimes I would go outside and sit in her and pretend that I was driving, listening to Elvis through the little holes in the dash as he sang, "Reach out to Jesus."

Eventually, I sold Betty to my Uncle Obie, who promised to fix her up and take good care of her. "If you just let it sit there, Guy, it is going to rust away," he said. And he was right, although I hated to admit it.

Twelve years passed. I seldom saw Uncle Obie and had no idea whether or not he had ever restored Betty. I was visiting with him at a family wedding. I was afraid to ask, but I had to know. "Whatever happened to Betty?"

"Betty who?" he answered.

My heart sank. He didn't even remember the car. No doubt she was dead and buried.

"Did you ever get it fixed up and running again?" I had a lump in my throat.

"Are you talking about the big, old '54 green Buick you sold me?"

"Yes," I answered, "my grandpa and I always called it Betty."

"I've still got her," he said. "Fixed her up and she still runs pretty well."

I didn't speak. I stood transfixed. Betty was still alive. Obie stared at me. It was like he looked into me and then he hesitatingly asked: "Do you want to buy her back? I'll sell her to you for $100." By nightfall Betty was parked in our yard in Brainerd. She was with *me*, where she belonged!

I drove her off and on for several years after that, but then major things started to go wrong again. I didn't have the heart to junk her, but neither did I have the money to get her fixed.

◆

We reach an age where the idealism of childhood confronts the hard realities of life.

◆

Can you believe I still rent a garage where I store Betty?

Sentimental, feeler me. I sometimes just go and look at her.

Sometimes I sit in her. When I sit behind her big wheel, I'm a kid again. My first car. I'm on my way to the basketball game between the Staples Cardinals and the Wadena Indians.

And then I'm younger still. I'm riding in Betty and Grandpa Guy is driving. We make our customary stop at the drive-in for a couple of "Black Cows".

The reality is I look down at Betty's floor. I can see the cement garage floor through the rusted holes. How much money will it take to get her running again?

Why can't I just let go?

I tried to ignore the weird sounds Betty made the day her

brakes died, but they died nonetheless. I can try to ignore the holes in Betty's floor or the fact that her engine is just about ready to fall out, but my attempts at avoiding these real problems will not make them go away. In fact, as the years go by and Betty sits in her rented garage, she continues to rust more and more.

◆

Only when we face the truth can we begin the journey into abundant life, the journey of sainthood.

◆

And so it is with life. We reach an age where the idealism of childhood confronts the hard realities of life. We are exposed to things as they really have been and as they really are. We can deny the reality and live a life filled with delusion, or we can face the truth with all of its painful consequences. Only when we face the truth can we begin the journey into abundant life, the journey of sainthood.

What is the truth? The truth is many of us approach middle age and discover that we have "great big holes" inside—holes even bigger than the ones in Betty's floor. We feel like something is missing. We *know* something is missing and we begin to search for it. We call this event a "mid-life crisis."

Many people have been "religious" for a long time, but religion hasn't filled the hole. Consequently, at this point, they give up on God. They have no real relationship with Him. They limit their church attendance to Christmas and Easter, if even then.

Those same individuals may have wonderful spouses and children, but the family hasn't filled the hole. *Perhaps a different spouse might,* they think. *Perhaps being single would be better. Perhaps just living together and maintaining my freedom would be better.* It is during this passage of marriage that divorce becomes most common. People ask, *Surely there must be something better than this?*

What is better? What will fill that big, empty hole in a life? Is it alcohol? Is it sex? Is it work? Is it friendships? Is it money? Is it things? Is it food? Is it death?

Hear Jesus. "I have come that you might have life to the full" (John 10:10).

Full! That means no empty holes!

But what do YOU do when you realize that YOU aren't experiencing the abundant life?

It's time to start over.

It's time to let go.

I accepted Jesus Christ as my personal Savior in junior high school. I've rarely missed Sunday school, Bible study, prayer meetings, or special evangelistic services since. In fact, I started working for a church as a youth pastor at the same time I started teaching. I've served as pastor at a number of different churches ever since. But it has been only recently that I admitted that I, too, had a big empty hole.

Remember, I told you that I'm a feeler and that I cry at television commercials? Well, the commercials that really do me in are Hallmark greeting card commercials. They usually go right for the heart and I'm a basket case after experiencing their overt sentimentality.

My sister, Janice, is a feeler too. Sensing that I was too much of a perfectionist and too performance oriented, she sent me one of those cards that reads like a sermon in miniature. The verse exhorted me to slow down, not to be too hard on myself, and informed me that I was a "wonderful person." I had a hard time believing it.

Being the perfectionist that I was, I could not think of myself as being wonderful. Can you?

Despite all the years of Bible studies, prayer meetings, and sermons given, and despite all the counseling I've given others, the fact was, I hadn't yet come to grips with what Christ had done for me. My focus always seemed to be on how much room there was for improvement.

We all have room for improvement. But stop right now and simply thank God for His great gift of life. Stop right now and thank Him that we are "fearfully and wonderfully made." Stop right now and acknowledge that because of what Christ has done on Calvary He views us as His perfect children.

When we come to grips with the full measure of God's love for us and accept it through faith, it is then that those big, empty holes get filled up. God's love is sufficient. It's all we need.

In order to embrace this love, however, many of us need to change our way of thinking. We need new minds. Satan, the joy stealer, has contaminated our old ones: "The god of this age has blinded the minds of unbelievers, that they might not see the light of the gospel of the glory of Christ, who is the image of God" (2 Cor. 4:4).

But Jesus, our Savior, wants to gives us new minds:

> Surely you heard of him and were taught in him in accordance with the truth that is in Jesus. You were taught, with regard to your former way of life, to put off your old self, which is being corrupted by its deceitful desires; to be made new in the attitude of your minds; and to put on the new self, created to be like God in true righteousness and holiness.
>
> (Eph. 4: 21-24)

Wow! Our new selves, our new attitudes, our new minds are like God's! That *is* perfectly wonderful! There *is* nothing to improve!

But old attitudes and thoughts die hard. Sometimes we try to keep them in a private garage (like I do Betty) and we find it very difficult to let go of them.

Earlier in this chapter I asked why it is so difficult to let go. The answer becomes obvious. Even though our old selves may be rusting and breaking down, we're familiar with them. We've lived with them all of our lives. Abandoning our old attitudes means we must develop new ones, and that's frightening. Where will those new attitudes take us? Change is frightening. Why not just stay with the status quo?

◆

When we come to grips with the full measure of God's love for us and accept it through faith, it is then that those big, empty holes get filled up. God's love is sufficient. It's all we need.

◆

When we reach this point, it's decision time. Will we make the journey or will we stay at home? Honestly, God wants us to make the journey, but in order to do it we have to leave home and we have to say good-bye, and saying good-bye means letting go.

Whenever we move forward we leave something behind.

Even as I write this, I am learning to let go. I'll share more about this is the next chapter, but for now let me tell you that my sister, Jan, was right on. I was killing myself with perfectionism and the need for approval. I could never be perfect enough or receive enough approval to fill that empty hole. I needed everyone's approval, especially God's, and it was God I always seemed to let down.

I wasn't experiencing joy in the journey. I hadn't surrendered many of the old worldly attitudes and beliefs brought with me from childhood.

As the years went by and I reached middle age, I discovered that all that extra baggage was weighing me down. I collapsed, again and again. My physical and emotional health suffered. Rather than getting rid of the old baggage I just got up and kept struggling on, sometimes barely crawling onward.

I have a new way of thinking now. My mind has been renewed, and I've put on the new self, "created to be like God in true righteousness and holiness."

There is *joy in the journey* and I believe God intends all of His children to experience it.

A lady told me about a close friend of hers—an alcoholic. "She never knew her family. She was abandoned by her mother at birth. She was raised by one set of foster parents after another. She never knew any security. Some of the people who took her in abused her. I think she has spent all of her life trying to find someone to love her. I don't think she can ever know joy."

What do *you* think? Is there any hope for this lady? Can she know joy? Or are the scars and hurts so deep they can never vanish? Is the pain so great it can never be erased? I believe that Jesus can fill this woman's longing heart if she surrenders to Him—if she truly let's go.

Letting go means lightening our loads and abandoning all the excess baggage of the past, especially the bags with the tags marked *guilt, shame, bitterness, and unforgiveness.*

Letting go means putting on a new self, "created to be like God in true righteousness and holiness."

Letting go means being transformed by "the renewing of your mind." It means a whole new way of thinking.

Letting go means dying to natural man, to our carnal natures, and allowing the Holy Spirit to fill our empty hearts and souls.

Letting go means praying, "Thy will be done," and meaning it.

◆

Letting go means lightening our loads and abandoning all the excess baggage of the past, especially the bags with the tags marked guilt, shame, bitterness, and unforgiveness.

◆

Letting go means forgiving and asking forgiveness.

Letting go means not praying, "Lord, give me all these things I need!" Rather, we pray, "Lord, give me what YOU know I need!" His grace alone is sufficient for our every need.

Letting go, we surrender our need for control.

Letting go, we realize that God's gift of freedom allows us choices. We can choose to love or hate. We choose to love all

God's good things. We choose to hate sin, and all that would keep us from knowing Christ's abundant life.

Letting go means bringing up the anchor and casting off, ready to begin a new journey in Jesus Christ.

Letting go means saying "good-bye" to the hurt and the pain and the emptiness. It means saying "hello" to love, joy, peace, patience, kindness, goodness, faithfulness, gentleness and self-control—the fruits that come from filling our emptiness with Him.

Letting go means we crucify old habits, old values, old thoughts.

Letting go means we can accept ourselves because of what Christ has done—made us "saints."

Letting go means we are free to be ourselves and can have confidence to know that we can enter the Most Holy Place by the blood of Jesus, by the "new and living way" (Heb. 10:19). That new way is the way of truth. It means that we can strip off our masks, quit playing games, and die to the survival roles we've played since childhood.

Letting go means we are free to love and be loved unconditionally. We no longer need to keep score.

Letting go means letting God.

When you get really desperate, you have no choice but to let God. When I reached that point, I wrote in my journal:

Prayer of a Desperate Man

I do not pray for a life untouched by pain,
or a soul unvisited by trial.
I do not ask for health for all my days,
or years that bring only smiles.

I do not desire riches beyond compare,
or a life in which I know no need.
I do not ask for the applause of men,
or fame that comes from noble deeds.

I but ask that You would keep me looking up,
keep me humble, keep me true.
I but ask that You would always do Your will,
no matter what I beg of You.

Though I may plead and desperate seem,
and of you selfish things I heed;
Oh, Lord, do not give me what I want,
give me what You know I need!

For I've lived long enough, Oh, Lord,
I know I know not what is best.
The faith that works, the faith that grows,
is the faith that stands the test!

I was a visitor at a Sunday evening church service in 1974. The pastor asked for testimonies and one by one people in the congregation rose to their feet. They spoke of God's working in their lives. Each testimony seemed a little more eloquent and longer. I can't remember any of the specifics of the testimonies, but I remember I thought they were an impressive witness.

When the pastor asked if there were any other testimonies, an old lady across the aisle from me slowly rose to her feet. She wore a sweater that looked like she had lived in it for the last fifty years. Her hands were rough and she held a handcarved cane in the left one. Her right hand clutched a Bible that looked old enough to have been one of the King James originals. Her face was weather-beaten and bronzed from the sun. But her eyes danced a merry dance, and her voice sang as she spoke: "God," she said, and then she paused. There was silence in the church. Just one word and yet her voice was filled was love. "God," she said again and then continued, "God is God, ya know."

And then she sat down.

No one spoke. I stared across the aisle at the lady. What a strange testimony: "God is God, ya know."

I've forgotten all the longer, more eloquent testimonies, but now, almost twenty years later, I still remember hers.

I no longer think it strange.

When we get to the decision point in our lives we must decide what we're going to do with God. Will we let go and let God be God? Or will we go the way of Adam and Eve and natural man and set ourselves up as gods?

Part of Exodus 20:5 reads: "I, the Lord your God, am a jealous God, punishing the children for the sin of the fathers to the third and fourth generation of those who hate me." This verse is but a section of the second commandment that forbids idol worship. Idols are anything that we put in place of God.

God is God. Not money. Not power. Not things. Not govern-ments. Not people. God is God. Letting go means giving God His rightful place in our lives.

People who haven't let go find it impossible to truly discover joy in the journey. They are always comparing themselves with others. They find it difficult to rejoice in others good fortune. They aren't happy unless they are the center of attention. They have a pressing need to have their feelings validated but have a hard time validating the feelings of others.

People who haven't let go see life as a series of competitions. They look at situations and ask "What's in it for me?"

People who haven't let go often see people as objects to manipulate in order to meet their own needs. They're quick to let you know when you've failed. They love to cast shame and blame and to persecute others.

People who haven't let go are very possessive in their love. They would do anything for the one they love *until* that person doesn't perform up to their standards. Then they punish instead of love.

People who haven't let go view nice things that are done for them as obligations needing an even nicer response. They view the things they do for others as debts others owe which need to be paid back.

People who haven't let go, haven't let God.

I've made a promise to myself. When I finish writing this book, I will decide what I'm going to do with Betty. I will either have her fixed up, if possible, or if not, then it's time to have her hauled to the junk yard. There are so many things from my past I have carried with me for years, but now I'm letting go and it is lightening my load.

It feels so good!

New Foundations

I n 1986 groups all over America were pointing to the schools saying "Get back to basics!" They usually meant that schools should concentrate on helping students develop math skills and learn how to read and write. I agree, those are basic and they provide the foundation that makes future learning possible.

But there *is* something even more basic than reading, writing, and arithmetic. Most of us receive the raw materials that we use in the building of our lives from our families of origin. It is our family of origin that can best give us the gifts of self-worth, stability, example, faith, and freedom. These gifts become the tools we use to build abundant lives. We've read horror stories of young people graduating from America's high schools not knowing how to read or write. There is simply no excuse for that. But what about all the children who "graduate" from childhood only to discover they don't know how to live?

Eva was a student in my "Developmental Reading Class." She always brought a happy smile to class with her, but the smile would disappear as soon as I called on her to read. She stumbled over simple words. She was frustrated at her inability to read smoothly and understand vocabulary. She was conscious of other students in the class who, she felt, might ridicule her. The reading comprehension test she took revealed that she was reading only at a fourth grade level, but Eva was a senior.

I worked very hard with Eva, trying to teach her the things she should have learned in fifth grade. She made great progress. By the end of twelve weeks another reading test revealed that she was now reading at a seventh grade level. Eva earned a "C" in my class.

Some would blame her elementary teachers saying, "How did she make it all the way to twelfth grade when she can hardly read?" And I'd be tempted to blame someone as well, if it weren't for the fact that after Eva graduated from high school, some employer might find out that I had been her teacher and accusingly ask me, "How in the world could you let her graduate from high school?"

It doesn't really solve anything to point fingers of blame. Instead we must identify areas of weakness and work on making those areas stronger. We must diagnose the problems and find appropriate solutions.

It is the same way with our lives. In the same way a reading comprehension test revealed what Eva's reading deficiencies were, God's Holy Spirit will convict us of areas in our lives that are built on crumbling foundations. It's not surprising that it is in the areas where we feel so self-sufficient that we often experience the greatest pain. God allows this because until we surrender those areas of our lives we value most, we'll never come to experience true abundance.

We should rejoice when we are convicted of sin in our lives, because this is God's way of helping us learn how to walk better.

Likewise, we should rejoice in our pain because it is often only in our brokenness that we truly learn how to lean on Him.

Equally as ironic is this statement of the Apostle James:

> Consider it pure joy, my brothers, whenever you face trials of many kinds, because you know that the testing of your faith develops perseverance. Perseverance must finish its work so that you may be mature and complete, not lacking anything.
>
> (Jas. 1:2-4)

Consider trials as "pure joy"? Only those who have actually experienced that joy can really understand. God is unable to fill us with all of His good and precious gifts when our lives are full of our own things. Mother Teresa said it best when she said, "You'll never know that Jesus is all you need until Jesus is all you have."

Unfortunately there is no Faith Comprehension Test. Our faith is revealed in the day-to-day circumstances of our lives. Those circumstances often reveal we have not discovered our sainthood and are not living the abundant life. Take a look around you and see all the hurting, lonely people who are desperately seeking something to give their lives meaning. Many of us, if we were honest, would admit that we are among the seekers. We should rejoice at this point because it is when we recognize our need and our emptiness that God is able to fill us. In the darkness of the night, God's light will outshine all others.

Many of us discover that we did not "graduate" from childhood with the gifts of self-worth, stability, example, faith, and freedom. No matter how good the home or how good the parents, no family is perfect. Some families are totally dysfunctional, not supplying any of the child's basic needs except food and shelter. The foundation that this child brings into adulthood is built on shifting sand and will not stand firm against a cold winter's blast.

Emotionally healthy families are much more likely to provide children with stable foundations, but unless the foundation includes a committed Christian faith the stability may lead to a false sense of independence and self-sufficiency. We have all met people who try to convince the world they need no one. Regardless, whether or not we are valedictorians of "the School of Childhood" or are desperately in need of remedial teaching, we must recognize that a foundation not built on God and His will for our lives is a foundation that will ultimately crumble into destruction.

◆

Emotionally healthy families are much more likely to provide children with stable foundations, but unless the foundation includes a committed Christian faith the stability may lead to a false sense of independance and self-sufficiency.

◆

Some recognize their dependency on God at an early age. Others carry their self-sufficiency to the grave. However, saints who want to live in the light of His abundance must allow God to shine His light into all areas of their lives. When God shines His light deep into us, we often discover that our foundations are badly cracked and crumbling. Some will simply add another layer to the outside, a new facade, and go on. Saints, however, recognize the need to allow God to build an entirely new foundation.

What about you? Are you experiencing the joy of abundant

living? Or do you just keep adding another layer to a foundation that really needs to be replaced? Tell yourself the truth!

I am not a psychologist but I know quite a bit about unhappy people who keep finding ways to hide their pain. I have been this type of person most of my life. I tried to convince everyone I had put my unhappy childhood behind me and that God had healed the scars of emotional abuse. I was quite successful. But I couldn't convince myself or those closest to me. My wife Tammy saw right through my facade and saw that although I talked a lot about the abundant life, I wasn't experiencing it.

It's difficult to write of these things that are so very personal. But I am willing to be vulnerable if my vulnerability helps someone else. I know many people think the best way to deal with the hurts of the past is to "forget them and get on with life." That's exactly what I spent twenty years trying to do, but I never really forgot them. The hurts were a part of my foundation, a foundation which was badly cracked. I discovered that it was time for a new foundation and I had to let God get rid of the old one.

When I ask my former high school teachers how they remember me from high school, most report that I was a very responsible, happy-go-lucky young man who would do almost anything to be the center of attention. I think they are right, except I wasn't really happy-go-lucky.

I remember that in high school I always felt I was on the outside looking in. I longed for a close friend and filled my need for intimacy by working harder. I was always laughing on the outside and crying on the inside. I practiced self-flagellation, beating myself with a wire clothes hanger on my fat thighs until I had large welts. Then I would take thumbtacks and poke them into the welts. I guess I thought if I punished myself, others wouldn't have to punish me. I felt great shame for being so imperfect. I felt God expected perfection from me and that I needed to punish myself when I failed to live up to his expectations.

Rather than an abundant life of joy in Christ, I looked at life itself as punishment. I had to be perfect; I had to take first place; I had to have everyone's approval; I worked harder and harder and won more and more awards and recognition, but instead of receiving abundant life, I only felt I had to work harder. I still felt rejection, and if I were being rejected it must be because I wasn't good enough. Maybe if I worked harder I could become good enough.

Cycles!

When I was about eight or nine years old, Johnny was my best friend in the neighborhood. I had the most fun when we were playing together. Johnny was being raised by his grandparents. I never thought anything of that at the time. I never did learn what happened to Johnny's mother.

One day Johnny told me that his father was coming to visit him. He said his father lived in another state. A few days later Johnny's dad arrived driving a black Volkswagen "bug." I can still vividly picture the car because, as kids, we use to play a game called "slug bug." Whenever we saw a Volkswagen "bug" we immediately would punch whoever was closest to us and say, "Slug bug, out!" Our eyes were always open for passing Volkswagen "bugs." Now here was one parked right in Johnny's yard.

After Johnny's dad had been visiting for a few days, he said that he would take Johnny and some of his friends to a drive-in movie at the Rand Drive-in Theatre near Verndale. I got pretty excited about that. I loved going to the Rand, and I thought it would be a lot of fun to go in the slug bug. But Johnny didn't invite me. He invited Steve and Rodney, two of his other friends. I remember riding my bike home, feeling as if the world had come to an end. Halfway home I could no longer hold back the tears. They were flowing freely by the time I walked through the back door of our house.

"What's wrong, dear?" my mother asked immediately. I explained it to her. "I want you to go back down to Johnny's house and ask him if you can go along, too." She was emphatic about it. "I can't do that," I said.

"Yes, you can," she answered. "I'm sure they'll let you go. He probably just forgot to ask you."

"I can't go and ask," I said.

"Yes you can," she said. "Go back down to Johnny's house right now and ask him. I'm sure they'll let you go along."

I wanted to go to the Rand with Johnny and his dad so badly that I believed my mother and rode back down the block to Johnny's house. Johnny came to the door when I knocked.

I don't think I've ever been as frightened as when I told him, "My mom told me to ask you if I can go along to the Rand Drive-In."

"I'll go ask my dad." Johnny said.

I stood on the step outside the screen door for what seemed like 20 minutes before Johnny finally came back. "My dad says there's only room for three kids besides himself. There isn't room for you."

"Okay," I said, but I don't think I did a very good job of hiding how deeply I was hurt. I couldn't go home and tell my mom. I was afraid she would call Johnny's dad on the phone and ask him herself. She couldn't stand to see me hurt so and would try anything to keep me from feeling pain. Ironically, her actions often made the pain worse.

I was riding my bike down South Sixth Street on the way to Miller's store to buy some candy, when the black slug bug went by. I pretended not to notice, but in it were Johnny, his dad, Rodney, and Steve. The three Milky Way candy bars and the bottle of Coke at Miller's didn't really do much to help the pain. I felt so rejected.

I carried these feelings of rejection into adulthood. One way to avoid being rejected is to avoid getting too close to anyone. Only recently have I realized how unhealthy most of my relationships have been and how hungry I was for genuine friendships. Despite tremendous success and popularity in the eyes of the world and even in the Christian community, I still felt like the outsider wondering why there wasn't room for me in the slug bug.

After I was chosen as National Teacher of the Year and honored at the White House by President Reagan, many doors were opened for me, especially many opportunities to speak. In 1987 I addressed a Youth Specialities Convention in Los Angeles and a tape of that message was sent to Focus on the Family. Focus on the Family aired the message over a period of four days in the fall of 1988. It has since become one of the most popular programs in the history of the Focus on the Family ministry.

The radio broadcast was followed by a film *Molder of Dreams* and the film was followed by a book with the same title. Both the book and the movie were successful, but I wondered what people would think of me if they really knew the rest of the story. What would they say if they knew I wasn't a very happy person inside, if they knew I often pretended to be someone I wasn't? Although long ago I stopped beating myself with a wire clothes hanger, I used a variety of different compulsions to punish myself. Work became my chief compulsion. Work brought praise and attention, but it was never enough. Although I had received the National Teacher of the Year award, it seemed I couldn't be happy until I received "The Best Person Who Ever Lived Award."

In the film and book *Molder of Dreams* I tell a story about an experience that happened to me in seventh grade gym class. I had never undressed in front of anyone and I was worried sick about doing it for the first time. In elementary school I remember Joe saying to me: "Guy, you have breasts bigger than most women." But Joe didn't use the word "breasts." The summer between sixth and seventh grades I took some of my mom's elastic bandages and wrapped them around my chest to hold it in, but I knew that I couldn't use the elastic bandages in seventh grade gym class.

That first day of gym class in seventh grade I put my supporter on backwards because that's where the tag was and that's where tags go, I thought. My gym teacher humiliated me in front of the entire class. When I'm speaking and tell this story, I've seen people fall out of their seats in hysterics, holding their sides, tears running down their cheeks because they are laughing so hard. But the audience always grows quiet when I talk about my humiliation.

Last year after I'd told the "jock strap" story for the millionth time, an older woman approached me. She waited as I signed some books and accepted people's thanks and praise. And then she shot out at me, "You're not telling the whole story. You're still in a lot of pain."

She took me by surprise. "How can you tell?" I asked.

"It's all over your face. You make everybody laugh and everybody tells you how great you are, but you don't believe them for a minute. You still think of yourself as the kid with the jockstrap on backwards. You are punishing yourself and it's going to kill you."

Her eyes totally captured mine. "You're absolutely right," I said. I was going to share more with her but the next thing I knew she was gone.

I can still see her face and hear her words, "You are punishing yourself and it's going to kill you!" I've wondered since if she were an angel.

At the time of my encounter with this lady, my compulsions

and my drivenness had not yet killed me, but they had raped many of my relationships, including my relationships with my family. I was taking Tammy for granted, assuming she would manage all of the details of the household. In the meantime, I was traveling about, becoming more famous and earning more praise. I also expected Tammy to be my mother and to care as much about my emotional needs as my mother had. At the same time I paid little attention to Tammy's emotional needs. I was too busy.

It was Tammy who could see that despite all of the praise, I still desperately sought approval. I suffered from tremendous bouts of depression, and on the days that I was home sometimes I'd sit in my office feeling the need to work constantly. Other times I would just sit there and cry.

My kids would stand outside the office door in our home afraid to interrupt me because "Daddy's busy." The picture of their eyes through the glass haunts me. It's easy to say that I was a practicing workaholic. It's much more difficult to say that I was a practicing sinner who had his eyes totally focused on himself. But that's what I was. I would try to find time to do things with the children and with the family, but if I couldn't find as much time as I thought I should, I'd feel "less than perfect," and when I felt that way there was only one thing to do—work harder.

Cycles!

During my bouts with depression I would think of some pretty horrible sins I had committed. I could accept the fact that God had forgiven me for them, but I couldn't forgive myself. Even though I would preach of His grace and forgiveness, I felt God's grace and forgiveness were for others, not for me. I had to *work* out my salvation.

I told people my depression was caused by the drug *tegretol* that I was taking for my epilepsy. It could have been the truth. I justified telling lies like this in the hope of earning people's approval. The more lies I told, the guiltier I felt, and the more my compulsions got even further out of hand.

I had developed epilepsy in 1985. Because I had been unable to totally control my seizures, I had not had a driver's license for four years. I told some people that not having a driver's license was

♦

Growth into sainthood involves identifying false beliefs and replacing them with the truth of God's Word. It is on the truth of God's Word we must build our new foundation.

♦

a major source of my depression. I told yet other people that my work schedule and many commitments were another major source of my depression. The truth is that these weren't my problem, but merely symptoms. Tammy reached a place where she wasn't going to accept lies any more. Finally she said, "Face it, Guy, you are not a very happy person, and you're not very enjoyable to live with."

That hurt. But sometimes we have to be hurt before we can be healed. This last year has been one of the greatest growth periods in my life. It has also been one of great pain. I had to be broken, and I know God may need to do some more of that yet. I have been receiving Christian counseling and am attending support group meetings. As I peel away the layers, the facades of my old foundation, I discover many beliefs that originated in my childhood. Growth into sainthood involves identifying false beliefs and replacing them with the truth of God's Word. It is on the truth of God's Word we must build our new foundation.

The journey is painful at times, but I "consider it all joy." It is when you surrender your self-sufficiency and lean on Christ that you will discover joy in the journey. One discovery that has been worth all the pain is learning how to "let go and let God." I had heard that phrase a thousand times but I had no idea how to do it. My old foundation and belief system knew a love that was manipulative, conditional, and performance-based. Imagine the joy of discovering a love that is totally free! I didn't think I could ever know that love. I wasn't sure that such a love really existed.

I know that my journey will never end until the day the Lord calls me home to be with Him. There will doubtless be many valleys, but I know that He walks with me. I have asked a number of people, including the Elder Board at Christ Community Church, to hold me accountable while I work through this process of reparenting myself. I asked Tammy and my family to forgive me and to have patience with me. I have asked forgiveness of those whom I have hurt through my manipulation, and I am taking life one day at a time. I have given myself permission to relax, to say "no," and to stop and enjoy life.

One important part of my journey recently took me to the cemetery in Staples. There, I had a long talk with my parents. I have no bitterness or anger against them. I love them dearly and rejoice in the knowledge that someday I'll see them again. But so much of who I am was determined by who they were and I needed to talk to them about it.

I am finally learning to accept the fact that I'm not perfect, and I can't possibly become perfect, and so I'm not going to kill myself trying. This has allowed me to listen to criticism without wanting to self-destruct. I want to pass on to my children the gifts a healthy Christian family gives: self-worth, stability, example, faith, and freedom. I want to help others discover those gifts as well—to discover their call to sainthood—their joy in the journey.

Did you know that Jesus has a slug bug? He does, and He has room enough in it for everybody!

Something to Believe In

E verybody has to believe in something...I believe I'll have another beer." That was printed on a T-Shirt I saw this morning.

There's an old African proverb that says, "It takes the whole village to educate a child."

As important as family is in furnishing the raw materials children use to build their foundations, the family alone cannot supply all of a child's building needs. To a degree, the entire village is involved.

The church and the schools are important parts of the community—the village. It is in church that children should come to discover their roles and exercise their gifts in the sainthood of believers. It is in school that children should be challenged academically and receive knowledge that helps them develop a deeper appreciation for the world around them.

Because many families fail to provide children with the gifts a healthy home gives, schools often find themselves merely "baby-sitting" kids with discipline and behavior problems. Real academic challenge is often missing in our schools. Too many schools have to concentrate on whether or not Johnny is a gang member and has brought a knife or gun to school. There's no time to concentrate on whether Johnny can read or write.

Unfortunately, many churches have only compounded young people's problems rather than offering solutions. Instead of standing firm on the Word of God as the authority and truth, some church groups have adopted worldly doctrines that allow for sex outside of marriage, the ordination of practicing homosexuals, and same-sex marriages. They have watered down the Gospel so that it "doesn't offend anyone."

Congregations all across America have split over doctrinal issues, have circled the wagons, and are shooting inward on themselves. One young man asked me, "If Christians can't get along on earth, how are they going to get along in heaven?"

Turning on the television I see a man who tells me he is looking into my living room. He closes his eyes and prays. Then opening his eyes, he points at the camera and tells me he can see me and that God has told him that I should send him my money.

No wonder kids are confused.

Of course, we must acknowledge that there are those schools that succeed and there are families that succeed. There are also many churches and ministries committed to standing firm on the foundation of the truth of God's Word. Thank God for them!

We must support them.

But remember, the entire village is teaching the children, and it is frightening what the children are learning.

Research has uncovered some startling trends. Note how high school seniors responded to the following statement:

"Finding purpose and meaning in life is extremely important to me."[1]

In 1966 over 80 percent of all seniors polled responded positively to this statement. In 1988 only 50 percent of seniors who were asked the same question indicated they thought it was of extreme importance to find meaning and purpose in life.

If a life with meaning is no longer a priority for our young people, what is?

The same society that still has the words "In God We Trust" on its currency, doesn't allow generic prayer at many high school commencement services. Groups such as the American Civil Liberties Union try to make the Boy Scouts of America remove the words "and do my duty to God and my country" from the Boy Scout oath and promise because "someone may find them offensive."

Duty to God and country is offensive?

At the same time abortion clinics continue to abort children into the third trimester of pregnancy. When asked what the difference is between a baby one day old and that same baby still in its mother's womb a day earlier, an abortion rights activist answers, "A woman's right to choose." It matters not that the child is alive, crying, totally capable of feeling. The abortionist pulls it from the womb, perhaps tearing off an arm or a leg. What remains of the child is put into an oven—a scaled-down version of those used to murder the Jews during the Holocaust—and incinerated.

This is the same society where it is a felony offense to destroy an eagle's egg. After all, everyone knows that an eagle's egg is an eagle.

No wonder kids are confused.

I see confusion in faces that cry out, "What voice should I listen to?" "Who can I believe?" "What is truth?" "Show me something to believe in!"

One day I walked into my discussion class and looked at the

kids. They were mostly seniors who would soon be graduating. As I looked into their faces, I wondered how many of them had something to believe in.

As much as I believe there is a need for rigorous academic challenge, I also believe there is need for effective lessons. True learning must not only concern itself with the head, it must find a home in the heart.

People learn in a variety of ways. Therefore, many different teaching methods should be used to accommodate different learning styles. Some students do best when the approach is all statistics, logic, and facts and is presented in a very concrete and sequential fashion. Others, like myself, are very abstract and random people who often want to deal with what is being learned on an emotional level.

I mentioned reading in college that "the world is a comedy to those who think, a tragedy to those who feel." That tied in with what I already knew: I am a feeler. I realized, too, that all people both think *and* feel, but I know that with me feelings dominate. On the one hand these feelings get me into trouble, but on the other hand, they often make me keenly sensitive to what is going on around me—the unfolding drama of life.

I showed my discussion class a picture of my children. "Repeat after me," I ordered, "Mr. Doud's children are the cutest children in the entire world." My students laughed, but most of them did what I had commanded. It sounded good to hear them say it.

Then I said, "Those of you who didn't say that have no chance of passing this class." They laughed.

"You know," I said, "I worry sometimes about my kids. I hear and know so much about the problems you face—all the different choices you have to make." The class grew very quiet. "Jennifer, will you come up here and be our scribe?" I asked.

As she came I said, "I want all of you to tell Jennifer what you think are some of the most prevalent problems facing young people today. Jennifer, I want you to write them on the board. Let's name some."

The students didn't hesitate. Soon the board was filled with a list that included "getting along with parents," "making a career choice," "doing well in school," "drug and alcohol problems," "teenage suicide," "changing sexual values," "loneliness," "sexually transmitted diseases," "teenage pregnancy," and one student said, "Mr. Doud."

Everyone laughed. "All right," I said after we had filled the board, "now I want you to select one of these problems and I want you to write about it and how it has personally affected you."

I elaborated on my instructions: "Don't put your name on your paper. I'm going to collect your papers and read them to the class, so don't write anything that would reveal your identity or embarrass you, but please make these as personal as you can so that we can have a meaningful discussion about these problems and how they relate to you."

The students began to write. When I collected the papers I was amazed by several things. One thing that surprised me was that most of them wrote about how lonely they were. The other thing that surprised me was that most of the papers were very personal and very revealing.

One boy wrote,

"I sit alone in my room at home and sometimes I get high. My parents don't know that I smoke pot. They think I just smell like cigarettes, and since both of them smoke they've given up trying to tell me I shouldn't."

He continued, "I lie on my bed and I listen to my

music. My favorite group is "Suicidal Tendencies." I like them a lot. Sometimes I am so lonely. I know that my mother loves me, but I'm not sure that my dad does. My dad has never done too much with me and since I'll soon be leaving home and going away to a Technical College, I don't think I'll ever become friends with my dad. I'd like to, but I don't think I ever will."

◆

And what I wanted to tell the kids, what I long for the entire village to join together in teaching them, is that Jesus Christ is that something solid to take hold of — that Someone to believe in.

◆

I read it to the class. When I got to the end of the paper, I was almost in tears. A couple of the girls in class were crying, and there was one boy who was doing all he could to fight back the tears. I said, "It is never too late to become friends with your dad."

Then one student who usually doesn't talk very much said, "I've never met my dad. He took off when he found out that my mother was pregnant, and she has never seen him since."

"Do you have a stepfather?" I asked.

"Yeah, I do, and he's a good guy, but sometimes I wonder about my dad."

"I'm sure you do." I said.

One of the other students asked, "Do you ever plan to look for him?"

"I don't know. He must not want to have anything to do with me or he would have looked me up."

"How do you know he hasn't?" another student asked. "Maybe he's been watching you from a distance. Maybe he's ashamed to come see you. Maybe he's afraid you will reject him. Maybe he thinks you'd be better off without him." And then he paused a minute and said, "That's the way it was with my dad. After he and mom got divorced and she remarried, he didn't feel like he should interfere in my life any more."

"But he is your dad," a girl said.

"That's what I finally told him," answered the boy, "and now I see him once in a while and we're getting to know each other."

Another student spoke, "I'm adopted and I often wondered about my biological parents. My mom told me she would help me find them if I really wanted to, but I decided I don't really want to."

"That's a very important decision," I said. "You may change your mind later on."

After a bit more discussion I asked my class this question, "What do I need to do to be a good parent?"

I can still hear many of their answers, "Spend time with your kids." "Practice what you preach." "Care enough to be tough and yet care enough to let go." "Don't talk out of both sides of your mouth. Be consistent."

I read other students' papers to the class, and with time almost running out in the period I grabbed one last paper. "This will be the last one for today."

I began to read:

> My family has been plagued with problems relating
> to drinking. My brothers usually drank a lot when they
> were in high school. Their grades were not very good,

and they all dropped out.

One day when I was at work, I had some visitors. They told me I had to leave work because of a family emergency. I didn't ask no questions, I just changed my clothes and left. On the way to the car one of them spoke up and told me that something had happened to my brother.

"Is he all right?" I asked.

He just shook his head and said, "No, your brother has been killed in a car accident."

I looked up and then continued reading this student's paper:

If the fact that my brother's death isn't enough on my mom, I might mention that my dad drinks very heavily. After my brother's funeral my dad decided to get a divorce. My mother started to drink. I'm watching her decay before my eyes. I told her that she's got to stop, and that if she continues, she's going to kill herself.

I looked again at my students. They sat quietly listening. I continued:

Two weeks after my brother's funeral, we got the autopsy report back from the examiner. We found out that my brother was drunk at the time of his accident. It was a head-on collision, and the steering wheel pushed through his chest and tore the big artery from his heart by the roots.

It's too bad that something like this has to happen to make people realize what they're doing to themselves and others. Maybe if people would take a hold of something solid—like faith in Jesus Christ—maybe then and only then will the troubles of our time be solved.

The bell rang just as I finished reading the paper. I hate bells! Hardly anyone moved. This time I had not succeeded in holding back the tears. "Those were his words," I said," "'Maybe if people would take a hold of something solid—like faith in Christ—maybe then and only then will the troubles of our time be solved.'"

And what I wanted to tell the kids, what I long for the entire village to join together in teaching them, is that Jesus Christ is that something solid to take hold of—that Someone to believe in.

Every Step of the Way

t happened in the bathroom.

Tammy and I were dinner guests at a friends' lakeside home. When I excused myself to go to the bathroom, I had no idea it was going to be a spiritual experience, but in that bathroom I discovered a few words that have helped me survive my journey.

The plaque that hung on the wall just inside the door looked like the one I had in my office, a plaque like the one my parents had in their home. But once I read past the first two familiar lines, the prayer took on a whole new meaning:

> *God, grant me the serenity*
> *to accept the things I cannot change,*
> *courage to change the people I can,*
> *and the wisdom to know that person is me.*

It is very difficult to improve on the Serenity Prayer. Next to the Lord's Prayer and the 23rd Psalm, the Serenity Prayer is probably the most recognizable and often used prayer. I'm sure you know how the original goes, but it doesn't hurt to pray it again and again:

> *God, grant me the serenity*
> *to accept the things I cannot change,*
> *courage to change the things I can*
> *and wisdom to know the difference.*

I love that prayer. I have always had it on my desk at school. One day a student commented (and it happened more than once), "Oh, that's the alcoholic prayer." And I would usually say something like, "Yes, many recovering alcoholics utter this prayer many times a day, but so do I and many other people who need to look to God for peace, courage, and wisdom."

But as I looked at the altered version on the bathroom wall, the prayer suddenly took on an entirely new meaning. "God, give me courage to change the people I can, and give me wisdom to know that person is me."

Most of my life has been spent waiting for God to change the world. I believed I was to be his number one helper. Yet all the time what God really wanted to change was me.

The journey into sainthood begins with God. But who is God? Paul Little in his classic book *Know What You Believe* says, "The word 'God' is one of the most widely used, but vague and undefined terms in our language."[1] I think for a moment about what Little said. Some people think God looks a lot like George Burns. Some see Him in a long white robe with a long white beard and a fiery look in his eye. In this era of high technology, to some, God is the master computer, the "pure mathematical mind." Conversations are filled with people saying, "Oh, my God" or "For God's sake." How many times a day do you hear people asking God to "damn" something? Shirley MacLaine tells us that she is evolving to become God. Mormons claim that people are "little gods" and that God was once a human being. There is a lot of confusion about God. No wonder we have so many wandering saints.

The Christian God is not vague nor is He undefined. He is a personal God who cares intimately about every detail of our lives, and He wants to help us discover serenity, exercise courage, and know His wisdom.

Even though He wants all of this for us, for some people he still seems far away. He was for Lisa.

When I first began teaching I was invited to speak to a youth group at one of the local churches. This church had set aside a special room for the youth and they had delighted in painting the walls in their own unique fashion. It was a motley room, the walls covered with a dozen different colors. The room also provided instant insight into who was infatuated with whom. All over the walls were names linking boy and girl friends: "Jon & Cindy," "Dave + Becky," "Scott and Lori," and the names of a dozen or more couples. The names covered the walls from floor to ceiling. I stood for a moment looking at them. I remember that one couple listed their relationship in a slightly different way than the others had. They wrote: "Tom + Sue = True Love." I smiled, wondering how capable seventh graders were of really knowing true love.

Then it caught my eye. Way up in the corner of the room above the door in the tiniest of letters, I saw where someone had painted, "Lisa and Nobody."

The room was almost filled with junior high kids now and the energy level was intense. Some adults can't handle being in a room with junior high kids, most of whom seem to function totally with their glands. Some of these Clearasil kids "fall in and out of love" twenty times a day. Acceptance by peers is far more important than what Mom or Dad think, and some kids would do almost anything to earn peer acceptance.

It's very important for kids in junior high school to have someone with whom they are linked—to "have a date." By this they don't mean going out on a "date." Instead, a "date" is the person to whom they are connected. Obviously Lisa didn't have a date. Lisa had "nobody."

The advisor of the group introduced me and the students quieted down a bit. The rest was up to me. "Do any of you know Lisa?" I asked.

One boy with long blond hair immediately answered, "I know lots of Lisas. Every girl in our school is named Lisa." And then they all laughed. A joker.

"I'm talking about that Lisa whose name I see up there above the door. The Lisa that feels she has nobody."

Everyone watched as I walked toward the corner where "Lisa and Nobody" was painted.

"Who painted that?" the advisor asked.

"I did," a girl answered. "I'm Lisa."

All eyes turned to her and there was a strange silence in the room.

"Your name isn't Lisa," the youth advisor said with a laugh.

"Don't you think I know that?" "Lisa" wasn't laughing.

There was a pause for a few moments. "I didn't have anybody in junior high school, either," I said. "I never even had a date until after I graduated from college and finished my first year of teaching. I couldn't believe any girl would even be interested in me. I used to weigh over three hundred pounds. I was fat. Even my fat had fat."

The kids laughed. They were listening and so I continued my story. I kept looking at "Lisa." I talked about the loneliness I had experienced. Other discussions with young people had revealed that loneliness was common among them and one of the ills that forced many of them to take drastic measures trying to find something to fill their lonely hearts. I knew from my experience with adults that loneliness was as real for them. Adults are better at hiding, or perhaps they feel more need to hide loneliness.

Eventually I brought the discussion around to Jesus. I asked, "Who is Jesus to you?"

There was a real uneasiness in the room. Even the advisor seemed uneasy. It was Lisa who broke the silence. "I pray to Jesus," she said, "but He doesn't answer. I need a Jesus with skin on."

I had never heard it expressed so directly. "I need a Jesus with skin on." I had to stop for a moment and take it in. When the discussion resumed, it revealed what I had expected. Most of these kids had not really discovered how to have a close personal relationship with Jesus. To them Jesus was someone distant and uninvolved in their lives. Intellectually they had acknowledged Him, but they doubted whether He really cared about their dates, their grades, their dreams, their aches, their loneliness, their pimples. If they could just meet Him with "some skin on."

I told the group about Henry Kopka who had been my eighth grade math teacher and senior high German teacher. Mr. Kopka had modeled Jesus' life style to me. He had been my "Jesus with skin." Through the example of Mr. Kopka's commitment to Christ, I had discovered that Jesus' love was real and was intended for me. I explained that we all experience Christ's love in the fellowship of believers and rather than waiting for someone to love us, we must reach out with Christ's love and love others. We must be "Jesus with skin on" to others.

I don't know if any of it made sense to them, or if Lisa felt any less lonely, but I was reminded again of God's personal love for us. In the same sense that we can model Christ's love to one another and be a Jesus with skin on, Jesus is God's model to us. Jesus is God with skin on. Everything we want to know about God is revealed to us in Christ Jesus. If we are going to know true peace, courage, and wisdom it is to Him we must direct our prayers. He is not vague and undefined. He walked among us and showed us the way. He continues to show us the way today.

One of my favorite preachers, Chuck Swindoll, writes:

> I am convinced that there is nothing more important about us than what we think about God. Knowing God shapes our moral and ethical standards; directly affects our response to pain and hardship; motivates our response toward fortune, fame, power, and pleasure; gives us strength when we are tempted; keeps us faithful and courageous when we are outnumbered; enhances our worship and prompts our praise; determines our life style and our philosophy; gives meaning and significance to our relationships; makes us sensitive and creates the desire for obedience; stimulates hope to go on, regardless; enables me to know what to reject and what to respect while I'm riveted to planet Earth; is the foundation upon which EVERYTHING rests![2]

Wow! Read that several times. It's loaded. That final statement is a sermon in itself. "Knowing God is the foundation upon which EVERYTHING rests!"

It is impossible to journey into sainthood without a close, intimate relationship with God. Many of us, however, feel much like Lisa. How do we come to know God with skin on?

The Serenity Prayer asks God for "courage to change the things I can." What can Lisa change? What can Guy Doud change? What can you change? The question really should be, "What will we allow God to change?" Sainthood begins when we come to a close personal relationship with Him and allow Him to change us.

◆

We all experience Christ's love in the fellowship of believers and rather than waiting for someone to love us, we must reach out with Christ's love and love others. We must be "Jesus with skin on" to others.

◆

Look at what Paul writes:

> Therefore, if anyone is in Christ, he is a new creation; the old has gone, the new has come! All this is from God, who reconciled us to himself through Christ and gave us the ministry of reconciliation: that God was reconciling the world to himself in Christ, not counting men's sins against them. And he has committed to us the message of reconciliation. We are therefore Christ's ambassadors, as though God were making his appeal through us. We implore you on Christ's behalf: Be reconciled to God. God made him who had no sin to be sin for us, so that in him we might become the righteousness of God.
>
> (2 Cor. 5:17-21)

We are able to have the righteousness of God in us! That's sainthood! It's entirely God's doing. *He* makes it possible.

It is because of him that you are in Christ Jesus, who has become for us wisdom from God—that is, our righteousness, holiness, and redemption (1 Cor. 1:30).

Although God has made this sainthood possible, many choose to reject it. In order to experience righteous sainthood we must live as righteous saints. John writes:

> Dear children, do not let anyone lead you astray. He who does what is right is righteous, just as he is righteous. He who does what is sinful is of the devil, because the devil has been sinning from the beginning. The reason the Son of God appeared was to destroy the devil's work. No one who is born of God will continue to sin, because God's seed remains in him; he cannot go on sinning, because he has been born of God. This is how we know who the children of God are and who the children of the devil are: Anyone who does not do what is right is not a child of God; nor is anyone who does not love his brother.
>
> (1 John 3:7-10)

I was talking with a man who simply said, "Pastor, I'm not addicted to alcohol, sex, gambling, or drugs, I'm just addicted to sin."

"Sin addicts" never really experience the sainthood and the abundance of life in Christ. They find it as hard to believe that God really expects them to quit sinning and live righteously as an alcoholic finds it possible to believe that he must quit drinking completely and live soberly. The task seems impossible.

Charlie Peterson was a saint. I never met a man who had more genuine love for people. When you were in Charlie's presence, you could just sense his love pouring out. He lived his love for Christ in service to our community, and many lives were touched by him. When he died, they named the community gardens after him, but some of us felt he was entitled to a lot more recognition than that. Each year I visit Charlie's grave, and I thank God for him and what his life taught me. Charlie Peterson was a recovering alcoholic.

When I read the eulogy at his funeral I told everyone that Charlie thought that the Serenity Prayer and the Twelve Steps of Alcoholics Anonymous were the two greatest things ever written outside of the Bible. "I say the Serenity Prayer a dozen times a day," he said, "and if you follow the Twelve Steps they'll help you discover true meaning in life."

The first time Charlie ever told me that I argued. I said, "The Bible is all you need, Charlie."

He answered, "The Twelve Steps led me to the Bible." I still have a copy of The Twelve Steps that Charlie gave me. I've known many recovering addicts for whom The Twelve Steps have provided direction and helped lead to recovery. Quite frankly, some of the recovering alcoholics I know are some of God's most special saints. It would be wonderful if "sin addicts," those who continue to willfully practice sin and never experience the sainthood of abundance, could follow some twelve steps of their own.

A few years ago, sensing this need for a step-by-step process for those who want to experience sainthood like an alcoholic wants to experience sobriety, I took The Twelve Steps of Alcoholics Anonymous and developed these Twelve Steps for Sinners.

TWELVE STEPS FOR SINNERS

1. I admit that I'm a sinner, born with a rebellious nature. I have no one but myself to blame for my sin. My sin has separated me from God.

2. I came to believe that only God through His Son Jesus Christ can restore the union that was broken because of my sin. This "re-union" with God is the only thing that can bring real peace and sanity to my life.

3. I made a decision to turn my will and my life over to Jesus Christ.

4. I made a searching and fearless moral inventory of the exact nature of my sins.

5. I confessed to God, to myself, and to a trusted brother or sister in Christ, the exact sins I committed.

6. I believe that the blood of Jesus Christ cleanses me of all my sin.

7. I humbly ask Christ to forgive my sin and to walk with me as I seek to grow in His image and in His sainthood.

8. I know that I must first "go and be reconciled with my brother," so I made a list of all persons I had harmed because of my sin, and I prepared to make amends to them all.

9. I made direct amends to all people wherever possible, except when to do so would injure them or others.

10. I continue to take personal inventory, and when I have sinned, promptly confess my sin.

11. I sought through prayer, fellowship, meditation, Bible Study, and obedience to God's Word to be filled with the Holy Spirit, seeking to know God's will and delight in it.

and obedience to God's Word to be filled with the Holy Spirit, seeking to know God's will and delight in it.

12. Having had a spiritual awakening as a result of these steps, I try to carry the "Gospel" (good news) to sinners and to practice these principles in all my affairs.

Shortly after I had written these Twelve Steps for Sinners I presented them at a Youth Specialties convention in Los Angeles. One of the youth pastors who was attending my session approached me at the conclusion of my workshop. "Wouldn't it be

♦

He doesn't want you to change the world, He just wants you to allow Him to change you!

♦

great if churches had support groups for sinners using twelve steps like the ones you presented?"

"Some churches do," I said.

"In our church it seems like everyone is trying to impress everyone else with how righteous they are. It would help many people to know that they are not the only ones struggling," he said.

"You sound like a man after my own heart," I joked. "Why not talk to your senior pastor and see if you could start a support group for sinners."

A few months later I received a letter from this youth pastor. He had been given the green light to begin the support group, and according to his letter many people had opened up and shared that they found it very difficult to live the saintly life of righteousness. "We are using the Twelve Steps for Sinners. I never knew there was so much pain in the people of our church," he wrote, "and that they had kept this pain hidden for so long."

What better place to bring your pain than to a church that introduces others to a personal Savior? His name is Jesus Christ, and He is God with skin on. He doesn't want you to change the world, He just wants you to allow Him to change *you*!

Cheers

It was my first trip to Boston. I wanted to see Harvard, Fenway Park, and the Boston gardens. My host said, "I'm sure you'll want to see Cheers.

"Is there really such a place?" I asked.

"Oh, they don't really film the television show here," he said, "but the building front you see on television is here."

After a few turns of the car, he said, "That's Cheers, right there."

And there it was—the building front seen every week on one of America's ten most popular and enduring television shows.

I blinked. I imagined I saw Cliff and Norm entering the front door. Most Americans know more about Cliff and Norm, two of the regulars at Cheers, than they do about their next door neighbors.

Cliff works for the United States Post Office. He's a mailman. Although he's in his mid-forties, he still lives at home with his mother. It's obvious that Cliff desperately wants to be accepted and that he seeks companionship at Cheers. He hides his loneliness and pain by playing the part of the "know-it-all" and is a seeming authority on everything, no matter what the topic.

Norman Peterson, better know simply as Norm, parks his over-weight body at the end of the bar next to Cliff. Norm is married, but is never seen with his wife Vera. He often pokes fun at her. An unemployed certified public accountant, Norm doesn't seem too concerned about finding a job. He's always good for a laugh.

Another frequent bar patron is Fraizer Crane, a psychiatrist. Although he is a Doctor of Psychiatry and helps others work through their insecurities, Fraizer himself is very insecure. To hide his insecurity he often appears to be a snob, and he projects an image of superiority over everyone else. It is obvious he desperate-ly wants to be "just one of the guys."

The bartender at Cheers is Sam Malone. Sam is a retired relief pitcher for the Boston Red Sox and a recovering alcoholic. He is quite the "womanizer." He sees women merely as sexual objects, and he sees himself as God's greatest gift to them. Relationships for Sam don't ever get much beyond the physical level.

There are, of course, other regulars on the television show, but Cliff, Norm, Fraizer and Sam are a good representation of the con-gregation at Cheers.

Each of the three patrons have their favorite spots at the bar and each week you'll find them there. Heaven forbid that someone else should sit in Norm's spot at the end of the bar! Norm is as protective of his bar stool as some I know are of their favorite pew at church.

I love the theme song from Cheers, but I wonder how many people have ever really heard the words?

> *Making your way in the world today*
> *takes everything you've got.*
> *Taking a break from all your worries,*

sure would help a lot.
Wouldn't you like to get away?
Sometimes you want to go where everybody
knows your name and they're always glad you came.
You want to be where you can see
the troubles are all the same.
You want to be where everybody knows your name.

You want to go where people are all the same.
You want to go where everybody knows your name.

Just where is that place where people are all the same? Where does everyone know your name and they're glad you came? Is that place Cheers or your favorite neighborhood bar?

Wayward saints...

Oh, for churches like Cheers! Bruce Larson and Keith Miller in their book *The Edge of Adventure* compare the local church with the neighborhood bar. Are you ready for this?

> The neighborhood bar is possibly the best counterfeit there is for the fellowship Christ wants to give His church. It's an imitation, dispensing liquor instead of grace, escape rather than reality, but it is a permissive, accepting and inclusive fellowship. It is unshockable. It is democratic. You can tell people secrets and they usually don't tell others or even want to. The bar flourishes not because most people are alcoholics, but because God has put into the human heart the desire to be known, to love and be loved, and so many seek a counterfeit at the price of a few beers.

If churches were places where people felt they could come, warts and all, and be accepted just as they are, we probably wouldn't have so many wayward saints. Instead, many churches seem to demand that we leave our troubles at the doorsteps and don our masks of "having it all together" before we enter. Some churches have gone to the other extreme and adopted the worldly value system that says, "If it feels good, do it."

Oh, for churches grounded on the Word of God, uncompromising in their presentation of the Gospel, yet with arms wide open to all the hurting, wayward saints!

Several years ago my wife pointed out to me a Dear Abby column in the paper. A lady wrote to Abby complaining about a woman who brought her two children to church in their pajamas. She said she felt uncomfortable around such "slobs" and didn't care to go back to a church that allowed such a dress code.

Abby didn't have much sympathy for the letter writer. Instead she commended the mother for bringing her children to church even if she had to bring them in their pajamas. Abby was kinder to the lady writing the letter than I think I would have been.

Church isn't a fashion parade. Church isn't a contest to see who can memorize the most Bible verses, or build the nicest building, or have the largest chior, or the most gifted pastor.

It is hard for some of us in the ministry to admit it, but most of the time hurting, wayward saints don't really need someone to quote scripture verses at them. They don't need someone to give them advice. They don't need to be told that they are miserable sinners. They don't need someone to give them a book to read or a cassette tape of a sermon to listen to. What they need first and most is simply to know that everyone is glad they came, and it often helps if there is someone there to simply put their arms around them.

A church flew me over two thousand miles to come and address their congregation. "We're trying to reach out to the community," the pastor said. Before the service began, I prayed with the pastor and the elders. Their prayers took me back a bit. They mentioned people in the congregation by name and added things like, "Now, Lord, we lift up Audrey. You know she's been backsliding—working at the movie theater, Lord. Oh Lord, convict her. Convict her, Lord."

I think I took everyone by surprise when I started to pray. I prayed, "Lord, convict me, convict me, Lord."

◆

If churches were places where people felt they could come, warts and all, and be accepted just as they are, we probably wouldn't have so many wayward saints.

◆

As soon as our prayer time was finished and the pastor and I were about to walk out onto the platform of the church, he said again, "It is really good to have you here. We're trying to reach out to the community."

When it came time for me to preach I stepped into the pulpit and began to read some Scripture. Immediately the pastor was at my side. He handed me his Bible. "Read from this Bible," he said, "I forgot to tell you that this is a King James only church."

My Bible was a New International Version.

"We're trying to reach out to the community..." That's what churches are supposed to do. But, if individuals from the community get the message that "I'm no good unless I use the King James

Version, or unless I dot my 'i's' and cross my 't's' exactly as that church says I should," you'll keep more people away than you'll attract.

Legalism has taken the joy out of the Christian life for many of God's saints. Those on the outside looking in often see nothing very appealing.

I remember visiting a lady a few years ago who was dying of cancer. I had known her as a very faithful church attender and someone who was always more than ready to serve. Now, on her death bed, I saw another side of her. She was frightened. "I'm not ready to go," she said.

◆

If we could follow all the rules, we wouldn't need a Savior.

◆

I tried reassuring her and read a few promises of eternal life from the Bible.

"But I don't know whether or not I'm going to heaven," she said.

"But you believe in Christ and have accepted Him as your Lord and Savior, haven't you?"

"Yes," she answered.

"Then why are you uncertain of your salvation and your eternal destiny?"

She started to cry. "I've never read the whole Bible from cover to cover. I haven't memorized many verses. And I've never tithed like I should. There are so many things I should have done."

Ah, wayward saints, so unsure of their salvation, finding it impossible to believe that God has really saved them. Wayward saints who look at their lists of do's and don'ts and live forever frustrated at their inability to follow all of the rules.

If we could follow all the rules, we wouldn't need a Savior.

I don't know who said it but I remember hearing it. I didn't believe it. He said, "Jesus Christ never called anyone a sinner." I got out my red letter edition and checked it. He was right. This person also said, "He did call some people snakes and vipers. They were the religious leaders of His day, but He never called anyone a sinner."

The Bible makes it clear that we are sinners, but it stresses that we are ALL sinners. So churches are really places where we "are all the same," it's just that some people have chosen to accept God's forgiveness, so freely given. That doesn't make them perfect, but it does make them saints.

Watch out for those saints who think they are perfect! Jesus had a lot to say about hypocrites. He said,

> Isaiah was right when he prophesied about you hyp-
> ocrites; as it is written: "'These people honor me with
> their lips, but their hearts are far from me. They worship
> me in vain; their teachings are but rules taught by men.'"
> You have let go of the commands of God and are hold-
> ing on to the traditions of men.
>
> (Mark 7:6-8)

And that's still a problem today—rules taught by men. These rules aren't God's rules, and they create a false image of what the church is and who Jesus is. It is this distorted image that people often reject. They'd rather go to Cheers.

I was watching a television evangelist conducting a crusade in the South. He waved his Bible and ran across the stage. "I want to talk to those of you who work for the tobacco companies," he said. "You can't be Christian and work for the tobacco companies!"

Rules taught by men...

And as much as I agree that tobacco is harmful to the body and everyone would be better off without it, I also know that statements like the one above create the impression that our salvation depends on whether or not we jump through all the right hoops.

"You must not smoke or drink or associate with anyone who does."

"You must not attend movies or go to dances."

"You must tithe and give an offering above your tithe to earn the Lord's blessing."

"You must attend church every Sunday morning, Sunday evening, Wednesday night and you must attend every special meeting of your church."

"You must read your Bible from cover to cover and you must recite scriptures and cite references."

"Your children must not be disobedient or rebellious."

"You must have a happy home."

And so on and so on and so on.

Rules taught by men—rules that keep wayward saints away.

The next morning I heard that the same evangelist who had condemned those who worked for tobacco companies had been discovered soliciting a prostitute. But Jesus loves him just as much as He ever did and there is forgiveness, no matter what the sin.

There is only one sin that God can't forgive. The Bible calls it "the unpardonable sin." Jesus said,

> I tell you the truth, all the sin and blasphemies of men
> will be forgiven them, but whoever blasphemes against
> the Holy Spirit will never be forgiven.
>
> (Mark 3:28,29)

What is blasphemy against the Spirit? The Spirit is God. The way you blaspheme God is by rejecting Him. The unpardonable sin, then, is really the sin of never wanting to be forgiven. Those who reject God reject His forgiveness.

Legalists often paint a picture of a God who has a hierarchy of sins. Some sins on the list appear unpardonable. One divorced man, who had been broken through the process of his divorce, wept, "I went to three or four different churches, but when they found out that I had been divorced you would have thought that I had committed the unpardonable sin."

◆

Churches are really places where we "are all the same," it's just that some people have chosen to accept God's forgiveness, so freely given. That doesn't make them perfect, but it does make them saints.

◆

Thank God for churches that hold forth the Biblical Jesus. You can't help but fall in love with Him. This story, one of my favorites, illustrates the Jesus I have come to know and love:

> Now he had to go through Samaria. So he came to a town in Samaria called Sychar, near the plot of ground Jacob had given to his son Joseph. Jacob's well was there, and Jesus, tired as he was from the journey, sat down by the well. It was about the sixth hour.
>
> When a Samaritan woman came to draw water, Jesus

said to her, "Will you give me a drink?" (His disciples had gone into town to buy food.)

The Samaritan woman said to him, "You are a Jew and I am a Samaritan woman. How can you ask me for a drink?" (For Jews do not associate with Samaritans.)

Jesus answered her, "If you knew the gift of God and who it is that asks you for a drink, you would have asked him and he would have given you living water."

"Sir," the woman said, "you have nothing to draw with and the well is deep. Where can you get this is living water? Are you greater than our father Jacob, who gave us the well and drank from it himself, as did also his sons and his flocks and herds?"

Jesus answered, "Everyone who drinks this water will be thirsty again, but whoever drinks the water I give him will never thirst. Indeed, the water I give him will become in him a spring of water welling up to eternal life."

The woman said to him, "Sir, give me this water so that I won't get thirsty and have to keep coming here to draw water."

He told her, "Go, call your husband and come back."

"I have no husband," she replied.

Jesus said to her, "You are right when you say you have no husband. The fact is, you have had five husbands, and the man you now have is not your husband. What you have just said is quite true."

"Sir," the woman said, "I can see that you are a prophet. Our fathers worshipped on this mountain, but you Jews claim that the place where we must worship is in Jerusalem."

Jesus declared, "Believe me, woman, a time is coming when you will worship the Father neither on this mountain nor in Jerusalem. You Samaritans worship what you do not know; we worship what we do know, for salvation is from the Jews. Yet a time is coming and has now come when the true worshipers will worship the Father in spirit and truth, for they are the kind of worshipers the Father seeks. God is spirit, and his worshipers must worship in spirit and in truth.

The woman said, "I know that Messiah (called Christ) is coming. When he comes, he will explain everything to us."

Then Jesus declared, "I who speak to you am he."

(John 4:21-26)

♦

Wayward saints are thirsty people who drink from worldly wells that only make them thirst more.

♦

Wayward saints are thirsty people who drink from worldly wells that only make them thirst more. The church must be the place where wayward saints come to find water that will quench their thirst. Notice that Jesus never once calls the woman a sinner. He tells her that she has had five husbands (that's a lot even by today's standards!) and is presently living with a man who is not her husband. She has been immoral, but Jesus doesn't call her a sinner. Instead he offers her salvation and a place in the family of believers in the company of the saints.

Later this same woman, who out of her shame had come to the well while the rest of the town was napping, brings everyone to meet Jesus. The People of Sychar exclaim, "We no longer believe just because of what you said; now we have heard for ourselves, and we know that this man really is the Savior of the world" (John 4:42).

This is a Jesus who attracts people.

This is a Jesus people want to follow.

This is a Jesus that brings out the whole town.

This is a Jesus who loves wayward saints and desires nothing more than to help them drink from the well that will forever quench their thirst.

This is the Jesus our churches need to proclaim.

Yeah, I can see Norm and Cliff heading into Cheers. What would it take to get them to come to your church?

Real People

Joe Plut is a real person. Maybe you remember Joe? He appeared on the television show "Real People" back in the 70's. Remember that show? It featured people who delighted in "doing their own thing" and doing it with gusto. Every week the show featured people who did amazing things. It was astounding. There were real people who could sing like birds. There were real people who could tie themselves up in knots. There were real people who had lived to a ripe old age. And there was Joe. What was Joe's specialty, you ask? Joe Plut was the "Mad Hugger." He was also my teacher.

The college class was called Creative Writing and I guess Joe figured that in most of us our creativity had already been stifled, because we spent almost every class session doing exercises that would help us take a deeper look at life. Joe would pair us up on occasion to do the exercises. That always challenged our comfort zones. There could be no cliques or little groups in Joe's class. We would write about our experiences and share our writings with the class. This took courage and trust, but we all performed for Joe because Joe's manner commanded respect. You either loved him or you didn't. You couldn't be neutral when it came to Joe. Kids flocked to his classes, but there were some who wouldn't take a class from Joe if their life depended on it, because, you see, Joe Plut was the "Mad Hugger."

Every day at the end of class Joe stood by his door and gave out big hugs. At first, everyone was somewhat suspicious of Joe, especially the football players, but after listening to the guy talk for just a couple of minutes it became very obvious, Joe Plut was a real person.

Groups began asking Joe to travel and speak to them. He obliged. He talked about being open, about getting rid of the masks that we wear. He asked why people are afraid to talk to one another. "They get on elevators," he said, "and they suddenly lose their power of speech." He asked why people are so afraid to love one another. He talked of God, of his personal faith in Christ. He spoke of the brevity of life and how few people actually are in touch with all that life is. And then he hugged people. When Joe finished speaking, people by the hundreds lined up for hugs, men as well as women, many with tears flowing down their faces. It was as though they needed reassurance that they were "huggable."

Of course, the media picked up on Joe. He was not an "ordinary speaker." His was not an "ordinary speech." Joe Plut was a "real person" and they named him "The Mad Hugger." Not only did he appear on the television program "Real People," *People* magazine did a feature story on him. But despite all of his fame, those of us who were his students still felt that he was our special gift.

Every day I looked forward to the hugs. In Joe's class not only did he hug us but we started hugging each other. Soon students and teachers all over the college were hugging one another. I felt more fellowship and openness in Joe Plut's Creative Writing class than I have in many churches. That's because Joe Plut is a real person.

Often Joe would come to class and have a reading for us. I've never forgotten one that he read. I've used it in my own classes. It was written by that great author, "Anonymous". Here it is.

PLEASE HEAR WHAT I'M NOT SAYING

Don't be fooled by me. Don't be fooled by the face I wear. For I wear a mask, I wear a thousand masks, masks that I'm afraid to take off, and none of them are me.

Pretending is an art that is second nature with me, but don't be fooled. Please. Don't be fooled.

I give you the impression that I'm secure, that all is sunny and unruffled with me, within as well as without; that confidence is my name and coolness is my game; that the waters are calm and that I'm in command and I need no one. But don't believe me; please don't believe me.

My surface may seem smooth, but my surface is my mask, my ever-varying and ever-concealing mask. Beneath it lies no smugness, no coolness, no complacence. Beneath dwells the real me, in confusion, in fear, in loneliness. But I hide this; I don't want anybody to know it. I panic at the thought of my weakness being exposed. That's why I frantically create a mask to hide behind, a nonchalant sophisticated facade to help me pretend, to shield me from the glance that knows. But such a glance is precisely my salvation. My only salvation. And I know it. It's the only thing that can liberate me from myself, from my own self-built prison walls, from the barriers that I so painstakingly erect.

But I don't tell you this. I don't dare. I'm afraid to.

I'm afraid your glance will not be followed by love and acceptance. I'm afraid that you will think less of me, that you'll laugh, and your laugh will kill me. I'm afraid that deep down inside I'm nothing, that I'm just no good, and that you'll see the real me and reject me.

So I play my games, my desperate, pretending games, with a facade of assurance on the outside and a trembling child within. And so begins the parade of masks, the glittering but empty parade of masks. And my life becomes a front.

I idly chatter with you in the suave tones of surface talk. I tell you everything that's really nothing, nothing of what's crying within me. So when I'm going through my routine, don't be fooled by what I'm saying. Please listen carefully and try to hear what I'm NOT saying; what I'd like to be able to say; what, for survival, I need to say but I can't say. I dislike the hiding. Honestly I do. I dislike the superficial phony games I'm playing.

I'd really like to be genuine, spontaneous, and me; but you have to help me. You have to help me by holding out your hand, even when that's the last thing I seem to want or need. Each time you are kind and gentle and encouraging, each time you try to understand because you really care, my heart begins to grow wings. Very small wings. Very feeble wings. But wings. With your sensitivity and empathy and your power of understanding, I can make it. You can breathe life into me. It will not be easy for you. A long conviction of worthlessness builds strong walls. But love is stronger than strong walls, and therein lies my hope. Please try to beat down those walls with firm hands,

*but with gentle hands, for a child is very sensitive, and I
AM a child.*

Who am I, you may wonder?

*I am someone you know very well. For I am every man,
every woman, every child...every human you will ever
meet.*

After he finished reading it, Joe handed out copies to the class.
I remember that I questioned the theology of the poem. Wasn't it a
bit humanistic where it said, "Your glance is my salvation"? And
"You can breathe life into me"? Doesn't this place the emphasis on
humans rather than on God?

I don't know when it was or how I came about it, but I've
come to believe that we do play an essential role in other people's
salvation. The Holy Spirit convicts, Christ saves. But we are often
the ones God calls to stand in the gap. We are often the ones
Christ uses to help others become "real people." The statement has
been made a million times, but that makes it no less significant:
"You may be the only Jesus someone ever sees." It is in this context that Luther wrote of our being "little Christs." What an awesome responsibility. Your glance, your embrace, your sensitivity,
your sincerity may be needed to help someone find salvation in
Christ.

Peter writes:

Now that you have purified yourselves by obeying
the truth so that you have sincere love for your brothers,
love one another deeply, from the heart. For you have
been born again, not of perishable seed, but of imper-
ishable, through the living and enduring word of God.

(1 Pet. 1:22-23)

Real people are purified people who obey the truth and have a deep, heartfelt love for one another. They are people who have been "born again."

Peter goes on to write:

> Therefore, rid yourselves of all malice and all deceit, hypocrisy, envy, and slander of every kind. Like newborn babies, crave pure spiritual milk, so that by it you may grow up in your salvation, now that you have tasted that the Lord is good.
>
> (1 Pet. 2:1-3)

Two words are our focus here—deceit and hypocrisy. We must lay these aside, along with the others mentioned. It's easier, I'll bet for most of us to lay aside malice and envy and slander than it is deceit and hypocrisy. Deceit is falseness, plain and simple. Hypocrisy is falseness too, pretending to be or to feel other than how we really do. Real people, real Christian people, lay aside deceit and hypocrisy.

Hypocrisy has almost become a laughing matter in the church. We have come to accept the fact that everyone is a hypocrite. I've told the story many times about the young man who had the following encounter with Dwight L. Moody. The young man told Moody he never attended church. "Why?" Moody asked. "Because church is filled with hypocrites," the man said. Moody answered, "Well, come and join us, we always have room for one more."

The point of the story is that Christians are not perfect, yet God accepts us right where we are. Unfortunately, I think that many people, hearing a story like the one of Moody and the young man, take it as encouragement to continue their hypocrisy. "Everyone is a hypocrite. Ho hum...so am I."

If you believe that God smiles on our deceit and hypocrisy, you have an entirely wrong idea. The Scripture is emphatic, "Rid yourselves of deceit and hypocrisy."

God wants our faith to be real. He wants it to be a faith that works. That's why it's necessary to tell the truth, quit pretending, strip away the mask, and face things as they really are. Beneath the

♦

Real people are purified people who obey the truth and have a deep, heartfelt love for one another. They are people who have been "born again."

♦

mask you wear, are you really sincere in your commitment to Christ?

A young man had been coming to our church for about a year. My only real contact with him was when we said good bye at the door each Sunday morning. His attendance was spotty and he never got involved other than the Sunday morning worship service. Therefore, I was surprised when he called one day and asked if he could come in and see me.

"I don't know why I'm here," he said "but there are a few things that have been bugging me. I don't think you can help me."

"Let's give it a try," I said.

"Well, I've been living with this girl for three years now, and ah, I'd kind of like to get married, but she doesn't think it is necessary. I feel kind of guilty about living like this, but I guess it's better than getting married and having a divorce."

He had opened up quite a bit and very quickly. I sensed he was apprehensive about my response.

"You say you feel guilty?" I asked. "Why do you think you feel this guilt?"

"Well, this isn't the way I was raised. I was born again when I was about five or six and I was raised in a good Christian home. My parents don't approve of the way I'm living and no matter how hard I try to convince myself that what I'm doing is okay, I feel something deep inside telling me that it isn't. I come to church here and every time you give an altar call I want to come forward, but I know that would mean I'd have to go home and do something about it."

"You feel like you're being pulled in two different directions, don't you?"

"Yeah."

"Be encouraged," I said, "but start to worry when you no longer feel God pulling on you. It is then that your heart has become so hardened by sin that you no longer care about God's desire for your life. Right now you still care and that's an encouraging sign."

He stared at me a minute before he spoke, "I thought I'd come in here and you would tell me what a miserable sinner I am. I thought you'd tell me to move out right away."

"I don't have to," I said. "You just told me that you know you are a sinner and that you know you should move out."

"No I—maybe I did." He looked down.

"You know what God wants you to do. It is what I want you to do, too, but it really will only count if what God wants becomes what you want."

"I don't think I can do it."

"Yes, you can, and God will richly bless you once you make your decision to be true to His will."

He stared some more. "I feel now like I can't come back to church here any more. You know all this about me and whenever I see you, you will just make me feel more guilty."

"Oh, no. I'm not making you feel guilty, that's the Holy Spirit convicting you. He hasn't given up on you."

He went on to explain that his girl friend wasn't a Christian and that she had no interest in spiritual things. He felt if he got serious about his commitment to Christ he would lose her. He listed a dozen more reasons why he felt it was impossible for him to do what he knew God wanted him to do. I listened. I shared Scripture. We prayed. He left, and I never saw him again. When I tried calling his home there was no answer. Later, I found out that he and his girl friend had moved to California, and I've never heard from him since.

One of the Scriptures that I had shared with this young man was Paul's clear explanation of how it feels to be torn between the two natures, sinful man and spiritual man.

> We know that the law is spiritual; but I am unspiritual, sold as a slave to sin. I do not understand what I do. For what I want to do I do not do, but what I hate I do. And if I do what I do not want to do, I agree that the law is good. As it is, it is no longer I myself who do it, but it is sin living in me. I know that nothing good lives in me, that is, in my sinful nature. For I have the desire to do what is good, but I cannot carry it out. For what I do is not the good I want to do; no, the evil I do not want to do—this I keep on doing. Now if I do what I do not want to do, it is no longer I who do it, but it is sin living in me that does it.
>
> (Rom. 7:14-20)

This young man could identify with Paul. So can everyone who really seeks to do the will of God. Paul was a real person, a real Christian, who admitted he was struggling in an attempt to gain victory over his sinful nature.

Paul continued:

> So I find this law at work: When I want to do good, evil is right there with me. For in my inner being I delight in God's law; but I see another law at work in the members of my body, waging war against the law of my mind and making me a prisoner of the law of sin at work within my members. What a wretched man I am! Who will rescue me from this body of death?
>
> (Rom. 7:21-25)

Wow! Can you identify? Ever felt like a "wretched man"? Admit it now. How have you practiced deceit, and in what ways are you a hypocrite? What masks do you wear? What games do you play? If you are having a difficult time identifying areas of hypocrisy in your life, just ask yourself this old question, "How would you live differently if Jesus came to stay in your home for a month?"

I have to admit it, I cry out with Paul, "What a wretched man I am!" And I also ask his desperate question, "Who will rescue me from this body of death?" Ah, listen to the answer!

> Thanks be to God—through Jesus Christ our Lord!
>
> (Rom. 7:25)

Christ is the one who is ready to come and rescue us, and when we allow him to...

> Therefore, there is now no condemnation for those who are in Christ Jesus, because through Christ Jesus

the law of the Spirit of life set me free from the law of
sin and death

(Rom. 8:1-2).

Oh, read that verse to me again and again!
No condemnation!
No condemnation!
No condemnation!

Can you picture this? You are sitting on Death Row. In just a
few minutes you'll be strapped in that electric chair and the executioner will flip the switch that will cause your blood to boil. The
chaplain enters your cell. He prays with you for the salvation of
your soul. The warden appears and tells you it is time to go. You
rise from your bunk and walk down the lonely hall to the room
where the chair waits. They strap you in. All the electrodes are in
place. The doctor and the mortician wait behind the glass. This is it.

"Any final words?" The warden asks.

You want to explain that you don't know why you did so
many of the horrible things you did. But the time for excuses is
past. You want to ask for one more chance, but you've exhausted
your supply of chances. This is it.

The executioner puts his hand on the switch. You close your
eyes. You grit your teeth. Your body is tense. Your heart beats
rapidly. A million thoughts go through your mind. Then you hear
the voice: "Stop! Stop this execution! Let him go free! His debt has
been paid! There is no condemnation of this man. He has been
completely forgiven."

You open your eyes and there stands Jesus. You've never seen
such love in anyone's eyes. There are scars on His head from the
thorns and holes through His hands from the nails, but oh, the

love in His eyes!

The prison guards quickly removes the wires. They undo the straps. Is this a dream? No, there stands Jesus with love in His eyes. He holds out His hand. "Come, put your hand in mine. Walk with me."

No condemnation!
No condemnation!
No condemnation—"to those who are in Christ Jesus!"

What does it mean "to be in Christ Jesus"?

Jesus stands with his hand extended to me asking me to join Him in the journey. If I extend my hand to Him and trust Him to lead my way I am "in Christ Jesus."

To be "in Christ Jesus" is to give him my hands, my mind, and my heart.

To be "in Christ Jesus" is to rid myself of malice, deceit, hypocrisy, envy and slander, to become a real person.

To be "in Christ Jesus" is to die to the sinful nature in which I was born and to be born again and accept my place in the sainthood of believers.

To be "in Christ Jesus" means we belong to Him—and we are His disciples.

Disciples have to be real people.

Let me ask, are you His disciple, dear reader? There are over 70 million of us in the United States alone who claim to be His disciples, who claim a "born again" experience.

Seventy million! I can't help but wonder how many of us who are included in that number are real disciples. William Iverson writing in *Christianity Today* wryly observes: "A pound of meat would surely be affected by a quarter pound of salt. If this is real Christianity, the 'salt of the earth,' where is the effect of which Jesus spoke?"[1]

Imagine a one-pound beef steak (the United States of America). Now, dump one quarter of a pound of salt (evangelical Christians) on that steak. Will the salt make a difference? It should make a significant difference.

In his book *Disciple,* Juan Carlos Ortiz suggests that there is a modern Gospel—the fifth gospel—"The Gospel According to the Saints Evangelicals." Ortiz believes that this "fifth" Gospel is taken from verses here and there in the other four Gospels. Ortiz says, and I agree, that we take all the verses we like, all the verses that offer something or promise us something, while we forget the other verses that present the demands of Jesus—the demands of discipleship.[2]

Think about it. The church has done a wonderful job of adding members to its roles. We confirm and baptize and marry millions of people each year. We build more and more buildings, giant monuments to "successful ministry" programs. "Mega-churches" are now equipped with their own racquetball courts and health clubs, daycare centers, counseling centers, bookstores, gymnasiums. These churches are known as "full-service churches" and advertise themselves as "your one-stop church headquarters."

Yes, we've done a good job of equipping our buildings, but how good a job have we done equipping the saints?

Jesus commanded, "Therefore go and make disciples of all nations, baptizing them in the name of the Father and of the Son and of the Holy Spirit, and teaching them to obey everything I have commanded you" (Matt. 28: 19-20).

Look at the above verse. We've done a good job of baptizing, but how good a job have we done in teaching the saints **TO OBEY** everything Christ commanded? Ortiz calls this "the great omission to the Great Commission."

A book that really shook me up was written by Dallas Willard.

It was called *The Spirit of the Disciplines.* Willard writes:

> Worldwide evangelism has been strongly emphasized and also quite successful. Perhaps this has been the main task of the church during the last three centuries. We can be happy and thankful for the expansion of the church, both geographically and numerically. But our zeal and success in this area may deflect us from an adequate emphasis upon the understanding and practice of growth in Christlikeness after conversion. Have we done what is necessary to bring the earnest convert into his or her possessions as a child of God, as a brother or sister of Jesus Christ in the new life?

> Unfortunately, the answer to this question must be a clear no. Too harsh? Simply make an inquiry of your own. Ask your church, "What is your group's plan for teaching our people to do everything Christ commanded?" The fact is that our existing churches and denominations do not have active, well-designed, intently pursued plans to accomplish this in their members. Just as you will not find any national leader today who has a plan for paying off the national debt.[3]

You can argue with Willard if you want, but I think he's right. He goes on to say that after 17 years as a minister he became convinced that what Christians were normally told to do was not advancing them spiritually:

> Of course, most Christians had been told by me as well as by others to attend the services of the church,

give of time and money, pray, read the Bible, do good to others, and witness to their faith. And certainly they should do these things. But just as certainly something more was needed. It was painfully clear to me that, with rare and beautiful exceptions, Christians were not able to do even these few necessary things in a way that was really good for them, as things that would be an avenue to a life filled and possessed of God. All pleasing and doctrinally sound schemes of Christian education, church growth, and spiritual renewal came around at last to this disappointing result.[4]

A.W. Tozer warned years ago of "instant Christianity." Many respond to an altar call, or raise their hands while everyone else's head is bowed, indicating that they want "to accept Christ." It is a relatively painless experience. Just hold up your hand. (No one has to see.) There. Now your name is written in the Lamb's Book of Life. You're saved! But saved from what? What difference had the "born again" experience made in the life of the young man we talked about earlier in this chapter?

No. Salvation is a radical thing. It is a call to all that Christ has commanded us to do. Real Christianity will make a salty difference, in our family, in our waking up, in our work, in our relationships, in the way we spend our money, and in the way we spend our leisure time. Real Christianity is not casual. It is dynamic. It goes beyond mere intellectual assent to correct doctrine. Willard says:

> By the early 1970's most conservative Christians generally accepted that being a Christian had nothing essentially to do with actually following or being like Jesus. It was readily admitted that most "Christians" did

not really follow him and were not really like him. 'Christians aren't perfect, just forgiven' became the popular bumper sticker. (While correct in the letter, this declaration nullifies serious effort toward spiritual growth.) The only absolute requirement for being a Christian was that one believe the proper things "about" Jesus. Saving faith became mere mental assent to correct doctrine.[4]

Well, then, what is a "real Christian" and who are the "real saints"?

The Bible tells us that the believers were first called "Christians" at Antioch (Acts 11:26). Why do you think they were given this name? I believe it was because they behaved in such a way that it reminded people of the way Christ had behaved. They had the

♦

Early believers knew that following Christ required doing ALL He had commanded, not just those things they found convenient or acceptable.

♦

mind of Christ. They talked like He did. They did the things He did. They were His followers and that meant so much more than just agreeing intellectually with the things He stood for; it meant that they actively practiced the things He preached.

The early believers followed despite all the persecution they had to endure. They knew that following Christ would almost certainly mean death. This is a vast contrast to many believers today who raise their hands and sit passively in their seats. Early believers knew that following Christ required doing ALL He had commanded, not just those things they found convenient or acceptable.

And because they followed Christ in all things, they grew in His image and in His likeness. They became known as "Christians."

Today the title "Christian" is vague, ambiguous and confusing. Mormons, who do not believe in the deity of Christ, are often referred to as "good Christian people." The title is awarded to anyone who belongs to a church or ascribes to an intellectual belief in a generic god. Christians can be anyone who is kind or moral. Unfortunately, the term "Christian" is as confusing as the word "love," which has also been cheapened by a loose society.

Real Christians who want to know real Christianity, who are not content with games and masks and only images of the truth, must rise from our comfortable pews and leave our "one-stop Christian service centers" and go out into the world and make a salty difference!

Our Lord needs no secret agents! Those who are not willing to confess Christ publicly are not willing to confess Christ. Perhaps acceptance of Christ begins as a very personal and private experience, but it can never stay that way.

Nicodemus sought Jesus out by night (John 3: 1-21). If he were seen visiting with the man from Nazareth his career would be finished. As a Pharisee and a member of the Sanhedrin he should have known better. What good thing could come out of Nazareth? How dare this man declare himself to be the Messiah?

But Nicodemus came. Alone. At night. Secretly, he came. He listened. His heart hung heavily on every word of this Master Teacher.

Jesus looked at Nicodemus. Oh, the love in Christ's eyes! He told Nicodemus plainly, "You must be born again."

Scripture tells us that it was Nicodemus who stood up for Christ in the Sanhedrin when this religious body plotted against the Savior (John 7:50-52). Nicodemus was a secret follower no longer. He was there, too, when Christ's body was anointed and prepared for burial (John 19:39). This "born again" believer followed His Lord to the grave, and although Scripture does not report it, I believe Nicodemus was there to see the empty tomb. He stood staring into the emptiness, tears of joy flowing down his cheeks. Nicodemus became a real disciple.

◆

The development into Christlikeness comes through surrender to God's will, exercising the spiritual disciplines, and service to the Kingdom of God.

◆

Nicodemus did so much more than just ascribe intellectually to the teaching of Christ. He repented. He changed his way of thinking. He changed his beliefs. He changed his values. He became a new creature. He was not yet Christlike, but his new birth made it possible for him to grow and develop into Christlikeness.

The development into Christlikeness comes through surrender to God's will, exercising the spiritual disciplines, and service to the Kingdom of God.

I want to be "real people." I'm not content to just pretend to be a dedicated Christian. I want others to see Christ alive in me. How about you? Can you join in with me on this old American folk melody and really mean it?

Lord, I want to be a Christian in my heart,
  in my heart,
Lord, I want to be a Christian in my heart.
Lord, I want to be like Jesus in my heart,
  in my heart,
Lord, I want to be like Jesus in my heart.

The whole world sits strapped in the chair. Satan is about to flip the switch. Then, in walks Jesus.

Oh, the love in those eyes!

The Destination

Dead End

The black hearse turned the corner and headed down the street toward the cemetery. I rode in it along with some of the other pallbearers. The sign just about a block before the main gate read, "Dead End." The street *was* a dead end street and I'm sure the city street department was just doing its job, but at this moment the sign could just as well have been neon and flashing.

This was the end--*a dead end*. "How insensitive," I thought, and made a mental note to call the street department the following day and tell them about the sign.

Another time, in another hearse, on the way to another cemetery, to bury another friend, I had another unusual experience. About three miles out of town and about one mile from the cemetery, the hearse broke down. It coughed, choked, let off steam, and then died. Six of us sat in the hearse with the casket. No one suggested we hitchhike.

Finally, not knowing what else to do, we all got out of the hearse—except, of course, our dead friend. We stood helpless alongside this rural country road. The mortician who had been driving the hearse kept apologizing profusely, explaining that this had never happened before.

Moments later, a farmer in an old, rusted pickup truck pulled up in front of us. "I've got a chain," he said, "do you need a tow?"

We laughed about it afterward. It must have been a strange sight. All the mourners were already at the gravesite when our dignified Cadillac hearse pulled by a rusted, green, Ford pickup entered the small rural cemetery.

We figured that our friend just didn't want to go.

To be honest, not too many of us do.

The story is told about the little eight year old boy who prayed, "Dear God, what is it like to die?" And then he added, "I don't want to do it. I just want to know."

I don't think it's possible to come to peace with life until we've come to peace with death.

I've sat at the bedside of a number of dying saints. I've been there at the moment of death. I've heard the last gasp of breath and have watched the head go back, the mouth open, the body grow rigid. It's strange, the dying think they always have at least one more day to live or one more hour, or one more minute.

Not only do many of us try to avoid thinking about dying, we hate to admit we are growing older. My great uncle, Cecil Tooley, copied down some thoughts about growing older. I'm not sure where they originated:

> *How do I know that my youth is spent?*
> *Well, my get-up-and-go has got up and went.*
> *But in spite of it all I am able to grin*
> *When I think of the places my get-up has been.*

Old age is golden, so I've heard said,
But sometimes I wonder as I hop into bed
With my ears in a drawer, my teeth in a cup
And my eyes on the table, till I wake up.

Ere sleep dims my eyes I say to myself:
"Is there anything else I can lay on the shelf?"
And I'm happy to say, as I close my door
My friends are the same, perhaps even more.

When I was a young thing, my slippers were red,
I could kick up my heels as high as my head.
Now when I was older, my slippers were blue,
But still I could dance the whole night through.

Now I'm older still, my slippers are black,
I walk to the store and puff my way back.
The reason I know, my youth is all spent,
Is my get-up-and-go has got up and went!

But really, I don't mind when I think with a grin
Of all the grand places my get-up has been.
Since I have retired from life's competition
I busy myself with complete repetition.

I get up each morning and dust off my wits,
Pick up the paper and read the "obits."
If my name is missing, I know I'm not dead,
So I eat a good breakfast and go back to bed.

Author unknown

Have you ever read the obituary column only to breathe a sigh of relief to see that your name isn't found there? Ever check the age of those in the obits to compare them with your own?

I've had many good discussions with students about these verses from Sir Thomas Gray.

Elegy Written in a Country Churchyard.

> *The boast of heraldy, the pomp of*
> *pow'r,*
> *And all that beauty, all that wealth*
> *e'er gave,*
> *Await alike th' inevitable hour,*
> *The paths of glory lead but to the*
> *grave!*

Can you see the path that leads to the grave? Is it a dead end? One thing for sure, when we die we leave behind all we have. (Oh, yeah, I know, I also read about the lady who was buried in her Cadillac convertible, but I don't think she's going to get very far.) Scripture tells us very plainly, "For we brought nothing into the world, and we can take nothing out of it" (1 Tim. 6:7).

I was just a kid when I first heard Reverend Olson tell the story, but I've never forgotten it. I don't remember the details Pastor Olson used, so I'll make up my own. The story went something like this:

He was excited about graduating from high school and going on to college. He had his life all planned out, or so he thought. Then, one day as he was leaving his church after the Sunday morning service, he felt a pull on his arm. He turned. There stood an old man who stared him straight in the eye. "Bobby, can I talk with you for a few minutes?"

Bobby couldn't understand what the old guy wanted with him. He really didn't know him very well. They had never talked at any length before. He couldn't even remember the man's name. Besides, he was in kind of a hurry. He had to get home and get changed so he could go to work. He had been working since ninth grade, saving money for college and making car payments.

"I'm in a hurry today," Bobby answered, but the old guy didn't let go of his arm.

"It'll only take a few minutes, Bobby. I really would like to talk with you." He was almost pleading now.

"What do you want to talk about?" Bobby asked curiously.

"I know you don't know me very well, Bobby, but I've watched you ever since you were a baby. I've watched you grow up. I remember the day your parents had you dedicated. I remember the day you were baptized. I remember you in the children's Christmas pageants. You always spoke up good and loud. I've seen a few of your basketball games at the school, too. You always play with a lot of gusto." And then he laughed before growing serious again. "You're a fine young man, Bobby, and I respect you. I wish you nothing but the best in life."

"Well, thank you," Bobby said, somewhat overwhelmed at the thought that the old man had been watching him his entire life. "What is your name, again?"

The old man introduced himself and then said, "I know that now that you're graduating from high school you probably won't be home much any more, and I suppose I won't see much of you. I just wanted to ask you what your plans are after graduation."

Bobby had heard that question a hundred times the last few

months so he quickly gave his stock answer. "I'm going to the University where I plan to major in political science."

The old man never took his eyes off Bobby. "Good," he said. "Then what?"

"Well, I plan to go on to law school. I would like to practice criminal law. It fascinates me."

"Good," said the old man, "then what?"

"Hopefully, I'll join a law firm and establish a practice," Bobby answered.

"You'll be a good lawyer, Bobby," the old man said. And then he laughed and added, "We need good lawyers."

There was a momentary pause and then the old man who had not taken his eyes off Bobby's asked again, "Then what, Bobby?"

Bobby smiled. "Well, I would like to get married and have five or six children. I've always wanted a big family."

The old man laughed, "That will keep you very busy, Bobby. You'll have to have a very special wife." Again the pause before the question: "Then what?"

Bobby had never really thought this far ahead. His answer came more slowly now, "I suppose I'll continue to practice law, be a husband and father, take the kids fishing. I want to learn how to golf and things like that."

"Good, Bobby," answered the old man, "I used to golf. Even shot a hole in one once!"

"Did you really?" Bobby asked.

"Yep! It was a miracle!" laughed the old man. Bobby laughed too.

"Then what'll you do, Bobby?" The old man was serious again.

Bobby hesitated before answering, "I wouldn't mind becoming a judge someday."

"You'll be a good judge, Bobby," said the old man. "Then

what?"

"Well," Bobby answered, "eventually I'll retire."

"Then what?" asked the old man.

"My wife and I will travel. I love to travel. We'll travel a lot. I suppose our kids will be married and we'll have grandchildren and it will be fun to go and visit the grandchildren." Bobby had never pictured himself as a grandparent before. The thought struck him funny.

"My wife and I never had any children," said the old man. "But we sure did love to travel. Then what, Bobby?"

Bobby glanced at his watch. He was going to be late for work. He was growing impatient. The old man was kind but he was tired of the questions.

"Then what, Bobby?" The old man asked again.

Bobby answered abruptly, "I'll get old, I suppose, just like you."

"Then what, Bobby?" The old man's eyes captured his, penetrating his soul.

"I suppose I'll die."

"Then what?" asked the old man.

I've read that in an old cemetery in England there is a tombstone that bears the following inscription:

Pause, stranger, as you pass me by.
As you are now, so once was I.
As I am now, so will you be.
So come along and follow me!

I also understand that some wisecracker placed a sign beneath the inscription that reads:

To follow you, I'm not content,
Until I know which way you went!

When *YOU* die, dear friend, then what?

I say it again, I don't think it's possible to come to peace with life, until we come to peace with death. Jesus came that we might have life and have it to the full! But is this all there is?

A man from the land of Uz asked the same question, grappled with the same problem: "What is the destiny of man?"

That man's name was Job and he lived east of the Sea of Galilee,

♦

I don't think it's possible to come to peace with life, until we come to peace with death.
♦

an area noted for its fertility. Job had everything going for him. He had enormous wealth, and the respect and admiration of his community. He was a man of integrity—a good man. But suddenly the reverses began. His oxen were stolen, his servants killed, his livestock destroyed, his house smashed in a storm, and his sons and daughters killed in the house. Job, however, continued to worship God. He cried out:

Naked I came from my mother's womb, and naked I will depart. The LORD gave and the LORD has taken away; may the name of the LORD be praised.

(Job 1:21)

Ever hear that verse? At how many funerals?

But the trials for Job weren't over yet. Satan visited him again, inflicting him with "painful sores from the soles of his feet to the top of his head" (Job 2:7). The pain was so excruciating that even Job's wife thought he would be better off dead. "Are you still holding on to your integrity?" she asks, and then advised, "Curse God and die!" (Job 2:9).

Then to make matters even worse, Job's friends came to visit. They were appalled at his appearance and could hardly recognize him. They had come to comfort their friend but ended up insisting that all of Job's troubles must be the result of his wickedness.

Job, wretching in pain, overcome with futility, cries out, "Remember, O God, that my life is but a breath; my eyes will never see happiness again" (Job 7:7).

And then Job asks a most important question, "If a man dies, will he live again?" (Job 14:14).

One of the first funerals I ever performed as a pastor was for a young man in his late twenties who had been murdered. A handful of people sat there in the chapel of the funeral home, their heavy eyes looking toward me. I stood in front of the plain, gray, wooden box--a welfare casket. There was only one small arrangement of flowers. I wanted so to say *something* to give them hope. I felt so inadequate. When it came time for the funeral message, I looked into the eyes of each of the few people and asked, "If a man dies, will he live again?"

No one suffered any more or lost any more than Job. And yet, from the bowels of despair Job cried out:

> I know that my Redeemer lives, and that in the
> end he will stand upon the earth. And after my skin has
> been destroyed, yet in my flesh I will see God; I myself
> will see him with my own eyes.
>
> (Job 19:25-27)

Wow! Henry Halley calls that "one of the sublimest expressions of faith ever uttered."[1] I agree. Is it your faith, too, dear friend? Do you know that YOUR Redeemer lives and that when YOUR life on this earth is over, YOU will see Him with YOUR own eyes? Or is life for you a dead end?

Saints who know abundant life in Christ Jesus exclaim with Paul, "For to me, to live is Christ and to die is gain" (Phil. 1:21). Think of that! Living *is* Christ, dying is knowing even more of Christ! We saints know we have a heavenly dwelling place,

> Now we know that if the earthly tent we live in is destroyed, we have a building from God, an eternal house in heaven, not built by human hands.
>
> (2 Cor. 5:1)

Have you thought much about the house you'll have in heaven? Can you picture it? God made it just for you. If you're one of His saints, you already have a home waiting just for you! Yeah, we saints can have confidence when it comes to death.

> Therefore we are always confident and know that as long as we are at home in the body we are away from the Lord. We live by faith, not by sight. We are confident, I say, and would prefer to be away from the body and at home with the Lord.
>
> (2 Cor. 5:6-8)

Yeah, we saints live by faith and we know that we have homes waiting for us in "glory land."

Unfortunately, the world is filled with people who live lives of quiet desperation, their sights set only on the things of this world.

In Luke 16:19-31, Jesus tells the haunting story of a man who fixed his sight on the things of this life. The man in Jesus' story was rich and dressed in fine linens and lived the life of luxury. He cared not that beggars sat outside his gate, longing to eat the scraps that fell from his table. And then he died, and in hell he looked up to see the beggar that had sat by his gate. Even as the beggar had longed for a scrap of food from his table, the rich man now longs for the beggar to bring him some water to cool his tongue, because, as he cries, "I am in agony in this fire!" (Luke 16:24).

◆

Unfortunately, the world is filled with people who live lives of quiet desperation, their sights set only on the things of this world.

◆

The rich man in Jesus' story was obviously arrogant and proud. He carried his arrogance all the way to hell. His was the type of arrogance that is commonplace today. Legion are the people who will carry their arrogance right into hell. We seldom talk about it any more. "Let's be positive. Let's emphasize heaven. Let's avoid talking about hell." Even pastors of evangelical churches avoid the topic of hell. "It might frighten people away." But I don't think we can confidently walk through this life unless we can confidently look at death and answer the question, "Then what?"

Just like the rich man in Jesus' story everyone will experience eternal life. That's the truth! Perhaps Job should have asked, "When a person dies, where does he go?" Scripture gives us the answer:

When the Son of Man comes in his glory, and all the angels with him, he will sit on his throne in heavenly

glory. All the nations will be gathered before him, and
he will separate the people one from another as a
shepherd separates the sheep from the goats. He will
put the sheep on his right and the goats on his left.

(Matt. 25:31-33)

Are you a sheep or a goat? What's the difference? Christ
explains:

Then he will say to those on his left [the goats],
"Depart from me, you who are cursed, into the eternal
fire prepared for the devil and his angels."

(Matt. 25:41)

But what about His sheep? They are the ones that hear His
voice and follow Him. What is their fate?

Then they [the goats] will go away to eternal punishment, but the righteous [the sheep] to eternal life.

(Matt. 25:46)

John, the Gospel writer, tells us:

I tell you the truth, whoever hears my word and
believes him who sent me has eternal life and will not
be condemned; he has crossed over from death to life.

(John 5:24)

Have you crossed that bridge, friend? You know, the one that
leads from the dead end to eternal life?

I tell you the truth, a time is coming and has now

come when the dead will hear the voice of the Son of
God and those who hear will live. For as the Father has
life in himself, so he has granted the Son to have life in
himself. And he has given him authority to judge
because he is the Son of Man. Do not be amazed at
this, for a time is coming when all who are in their
graves will hear his voice and come out— those who
have done good will rise to live, and those who have
done evil will rise to be condemned.

(John 5:25-29)

After death, then what? If your name is recorded in the Lamb's
Book of Life, great will be your reward.

Then I heard a voice from heaven say, "Write:
Blessed are the dead who die in the Lord from now on."
"Yes," says the Spirit, "they will rest from their labor,
for their deeds will follow them."

(Rev. 14:13)

After death, then what? If your name is not recorded in the
Lamb's Book of Life, John reveals your ultimate end:

Then I saw a great white throne and him who was
seated on it. Earth and sky fled from his presence, and
there was no place for them. And I saw the dead, great
and small, standing before the throne, and books were
opened. Another book was opened, which is the book
of life. The dead were judged according to what they
had done as recorded in the books. The sea gave up the
dead that were in it, and death and Hades gave up the

dead that were in them, and each person was judged according to what he had done. Then death and Hades were thrown into the lake of fire. The lake of fire is the second death. If anyone's name was not found written in the book of life, he was thrown into the lake of fire.

(Rev. 20:11-15)

That's judgment day, friend. I don't know about you, but I'm mighty thankful I don't have to face that judgment. You see, that judgment is for the unbeliever. Those of us who have heard His voice, we who are His sheep, are His saints. Do you know what Scripture says of our deaths?

Precious in the sight of the LORD is the death of his saints. (Ps. 116:15)

Can I add a few dozen exclamation points after the word "saints"? SAINTS!!!!!!!!!!

Uncle Cecil said that he got up every morning and read the "obits." As long as you are alive to read them, you can still choose to become one of God's saints. But after your name makes it into that obituary column, it's too late. You'll never have a second chance. Today is the day of decision.

Face it. Death is waiting around the corner for you, too. It could be today. Come to grips with this fact and life takes on a whole new meaning.

Wait a minute now, I have no desire to frighten you or manipulate you. I remember hearing those "hell-fire and damnation" preachers on the radio when I was kid. They'd scream, "Your soul may be required of you today! Are you ready to meet your Maker?"

Their theological emphasis used to turn me off. But you know, they were right. Your soul may be required of you today. Are you ready to meet your Maker?

John was an arrogant young man. Whereas his father and mother had worked hard all of their lives for what they had, John seemed to think everything should be handed to him on a silver platter. True, his parents were quite wealthy and could afford to buy him almost anything he desired, but what John didn't appreciate was the fact that it had taken his parents their entire lives to accumulate their wealth. John expected to live in the same fashion his parents did as soon as he graduated from college, which he was about to do in a few months.

John was often aghast at the smallness of some of his parents' gifts to him. (They could certainly afford more!) So he thought he'd help them choose a graduation gift by sending them a wish list of things he desired. He'd like a new car—a Jaguar would be nice, but he would accept a Corvette. He wrote his parents that if they'd prefer, they could buy him his first house in lieu of a gift. John's list was quite specific, and he hoped it would ensure a generous gift from his parents.

Graduation day arrived. His parents hosted a party for him at their home. Friends and relatives attended. There was cake and punch. John was anxious to see what gift his parents got him. He kept checking the driveway to see if that new car would show up, but then his father announced that John was going to open his gift, and handed him an envelope. John decided his parents had probably given him a cashier's check to pick out a car for himself.

Opening the envelope John saw the word, "Deed." *Aha*, he thought, *a deed to some property.* He unfolded the deed. His mouth fell open. He looked at his parents. He was speechless. They had written on a card inside the envelope, "John, because we love you so much, please accept this graduation gift and always remember that the 'paths of glory lead but to the grave.'"

The deed was for a burial plot at the local cemetery. It was John's father's way of reminding him, not so subtly, that the paths of glory **do** lead to the grave. Although the grave is every man's destination, it is not the end. The moment of death will either be the greatest moment of our lives or will be the first taste of eternal condemnation—an eternity separated from love and from God. Whichever it is, we will have reached our eternal home. The choice is ours and the time to make that choice is now.

Oh, I did call the street department and they took down the "Dead End" sign outside the cemetery. I'm glad they did.

The Day
I Died

It happened at the turtle races in Nisswa, Minnesota.

Although Longville, Minnesota, 30 or so miles north-east of Nisswa, claims to be the "Turtle Race Capital of the World," Nisswa gives Longville a good run for its money.

Have you ever been to a turtle race? Around here, some people think that if you haven't been to a turtle race you've missed out on much of what life has to offer. Horse races, dog races, car, motorcycle, and snowmobile races can't compare to turtle racing. Although racing turtles don't move as fast as the "Funny Cars" at Brainerd International Raceway just south of Nisswa, nor do they fly over bumps on the tracks like motorcycles, the excitement they generate is phenomenal.

The turtles themselves make very little noise, but those cheering on their favorite racer act like it is overtime at the Super Bowl. Have you ever stood for twenty minutes staring at a turtle just praying for some sign of movement? You yell at your turtle. You speak kindly to your turtle. You promise your turtle great rewards if he/she/it(?) will but start for the edge of the circle. You see, all the turtles begin in the middle of this big thirty-foot circle and the first one to exit the circle brings home the "laurel wreath."

Of course, I've never personally entered a turtle in a race. "Leave that for the children," I say. But as you watch the races, which are held right in downtown Nisswa from June to August, you soon realize that the parents care far more about the outcome of the races than the kids do. Maybe it's the prize money that's at stake.

Over three hundred people with their racer turtles assemble every Wednesday during the summer. Heats are held to eliminate the slow turtles. Most of the racing turtles are mud turtles. There are seldom any snapping turtles in the race. There are races for small turtles three inches and under, and there are special races for turtles being raced by people from out-of-state. How's that for hospitality?

Well, it happened one day at the turtle races. What happened was—I died.

A large, enthusiastic crowd was assembled. The suspense was overwhelming: Which turtle would be crowned grand champion and win the cash prize? Several heats had already been held. Turtles unable to cut the mustard had been eliminated. Soon the winners from the first heats would compete neck to neck, shell to shell. But stop for a minute, the loudspeaker announcer had a special news flash:

"Ladies and gentlemen," (was there a catch in her voice?) "I have a very sad announcement to make." The crowd grew as silent as possible. "Guy Doud, who many of you know as the National Teacher of the Year and the pastor of Christ Community Church here in Nisswa...Guy Doud died today at the Brainerd hospital. That's all the information I have. Let's get ready for our next heat."

Then they resumed the races.

Now, in all fairness, you have to remember that I wasn't there that day. I was dead. So I'm not sure this is exactly how it went or exactly what was said, but members from my congregation who were there told me this is how it happened. Of course, members of my congregation who were there were in shock. They left the races. They made phone calls. How had Guy died? When?

Soon it was all over town, "Guy Doud is dead," they said. He died of a heart attack. He died of a brain tumor. He died from pneumonia.

Earlier that day I had checked myself out of the hospital in Brainerd where I had been hospitalized for double pneumonia and exhaustion. I was scheduled to give a speech that afternoon at St. Benedict's College in Collegeville, Minnesota, about 70 miles south of Brainerd. I was also scheduled to perform that evening in the Brainerd Summer Theatre Production of *Man of La Mancha*. I had the lead role of Don Quixote. Since I didn't have an understudy for my part in the play and since we had a sold-out house, and since I was going to be appearing at St. Benedict's in the afternoon along with the Governor of Minnesota, and since I was feeling much better, I thought it was too important a day to lie in bed. So I asked my doctor if I could check out. He said "No," but I insisted.

Finally, I did check out of hospital. My doctor made me promise I would come back in the evening after the play was over. I signed a waiver exempting the hospital and the doctor for any liability and with the IV still in my vein, sealed with a heparin lock, I left St. Joe's and headed for Collegeville.

I figure I must have died on the way to Collegeville, or at least that is about the time the announcement of my death was made at the Turtle Races. By the time I got to Collegeville, hundreds of people knew that I was dead, but my wife didn't. Tammy, of course, knew I was sick and in the hospital. She also knew that I was feeling better. The call that came to her was a big shock.

"Tammy, you have an important phone call," said her boss at the Regional Human Services Center where she worked at the time.

She went immediately to the phone. "Hello?"

"Tammy," the voice said somewhat hesitatingly, "this is Bob Gross. How is Guy doing?"

Bob Gross is the Superintendent of Schools for the Brainerd School District. He wasn't in the habit of calling Tammy at work and asking about me.

"When I saw him last night he was feeling much better," Tammy answered, obviously taken back by Mr. Gross's call.

"Have you talked to Guy today?" Bob asked.

"No, I haven't," Tammy answered, "but you could call him yourself at the hospital."

"Well, I called the hospital," Mr. Gross answered, "and they say he checked himself out."

"Yes, he said last night that if he felt better he wanted to check out so he could go to Collegeville today and give a speech with the Governor." Tammy was still confused.

"Well, Tammy," Mr. Gross continued, "I don't mean to worry you, but someone from the newspaper called just a few minutes ago and said they heard that Guy had died. I told them I didn't think so, but I would check it out."

Tammy was very concerned now, but she figured if there were any truth to the story someone certainly would have informed her. "No, Bob, I can't believe he's dead."

Mr. Gross answered, "I'm sure it's just a rumor, too, but I'll call St. Ben's in Collegeville and see if I can reach him."

Tammy tells me the next thirty minutes seemed like forever. She returned to her job. Her fellow employees, noting the lack of color in her cheeks, asked her what was wrong. She answered, "I guess word's all over town that Guy is dead." None of her colleagues knew for sure what to say or do.

In the meantime, I sat on the stage in the Performing Arts Center at St. Benedict's College, wishing I were still in the hospital. I could tell that my lung capacity was severely limited and I felt myself burning up with fever. I didn't realize then, that my need to give that speech despite the warnings from my doctor was a clear indication of how serious my need for approval was. Beside me sat Governor Rudy Perpich, the same Minnesota governor who

◆

I didn't realize then, that my need to give that speech despite the warnings from my doctor was a clear indication of how serious my need for approval was.

◆

had accompanied me to the White House when President Reagan presented me with the Crystal Apple. It was almost my time to speak when a Minnesota State trooper walked in and headed toward the stage where we sat. Since the trooper was Perpich's chauffeur, the Governor assumed the trooper had a message for him. But the trooper walked right up to me on the stage, bent over, and asked, "Are you Guy Doud?"

"Oh, no!" I thought. "They've finally caught up to me!" Immediately my mind was filled with a list of things I thought the Trooper could want me for. Perhaps they had been monitoring my speed from the air over a period of years (compulsive people often ignore speed limits) and now they were going to lower the boom on me. Perhaps the IRS had discovered some discrepancy on one of my returns and they had sent this trooper to pick me up. Perhaps...perhaps...a dozen different scenarios flashed through my mind, and then I suddenly grew very ill at the thought that perhaps someone in my family had died.

"Yes, I'm Guy Doud," I answered but I suddenly felt like Don Quixote facing the Inquisition.

"I have an urgent message for you. You're suppose to call Bob Gross immediately." He handed me the message and exited the auditorium.

Bob Gross, I thought. *What could be so urgent that Mr. Gross is calling me?* Again my mind raced with possible scenarios. Maybe Gross heard that I was going to be speaking in front of the Governor and he wanted me to push for more money for rural schools. Maybe he was calling to tell me something positive like I was being considered for the "International Teacher of the Universe Award." Or maybe, oh no, maybe they had discovered that I really wasn't a very good teacher and they were going to take my Crystal Apple away from me. A thousand thoughts went through my mind as I went to find a telephone.

Mr. Gross answered. "Bob, this is Guy Doud calling, what's up?"

"Are you calling from Heaven?" Mr. Gross asked.

"Well, not exactly, but I am at St. Benedict's. Why do you ask?" I was amused at such a strange question.

"Guy, someone from the newspaper called and said they heard you were dead. It was announced at the Nisswa Turtle Races."

"What!" I exclaimed.

"I didn't believe it was true," Bob said. "I called Tammy and she said that she thought you were still alive." Bob was almost laughing now.

"How in the world can something like that happen?" I asked. I couldn't believe it.

"You know how rumors can spread," Mr. Gross said, "I'll call Tammy and let her know you're okay. Hey, please drive home carefully."

I thanked Mr. Gross and went back to the auditorium. I was in a daze and told the audience so. "I'm dead," I said to them. I could hear Mr. Gross' advice ringing in my ears, "Drive home carefully. Drive home carefully."

Tammy sat waiting for Mr. Gross to call her back. Finally the phone rang. "Tammy, the phone," said her boss.

Tammy went quickly to the phone. But it wasn't Mr. Gross. It was a friend who worked at the hospital in town. "Tammy," he asked, "how is Guy doing?" He, too, had heard that I was dead, killed in a car accident. Tammy explained what she knew about the situation. She had a very anxious time before Mr. Gross called her back and let her know that he had talked to me and I was still alive.

After talking to Mr. Gross and before going to speak, I called the local paper, *The Brainerd Daily Dispatch,* and let them know I was still alive. The reporter seemed almost disappointed. I've wondered since if they had my obiturary all ready to go. It's kind of a shame, isn't it, that you can't read your own obit? After all, except for their birth and wedding it's the only time some people ever make it into the paper.

Once the reporter realized I was still kicking, he asked me for my reaction to the reports of my death. I tried to quote Mark Twain, "The reports of my death are greatly exaggerated," I said.

Wasn't I clever and unique? Truth is, I wasn't feeling very clever. I was still in kind of a daze.

After talking with the reporter, I returned to the auditorium, gave my speech, shook the customary hands, and headed home. On the way, I encountered a fierce summer storm. Driving into it felt like smashing into a building. Radio reports said tornados had been spotted. Winds and gusts exceeded 70 miles an hour. It was raining so heavily I could barely see ten feet in front of me. The car crept along. I began to have doubts that I would make it home. I even thought, "Maybe I have died and this is what hell is like." I knew better, of course, but I was having trouble breathing and my fever seemed to make me all the more delirious. "I'm never going to see Tammy or my children again," I thought. At that moment I lost sight of the promise of eternal life, my thoughts were fixed upon the now. "I'm going to die," I thought. "In fact, everyone already thinks I am dead."

I looked up into the face of the storm. It was as if my car were dancing on clouds. I could hardly see the road, and although the windshield wiper was wiping as fast as possible, it could not gain victory over the cascading rain that fell like a waterfall over a dam. I wasn't thinking clearly, of course, or I would have pulled over, but I was anxious to get back to Brainerd and see my family. I wanted to throw my children into the air, hold them, and feel their soft cheeks next to mine. I wanted to kiss Tammy and lose myself in her embrace. But at this minute I seriously doubted that I would ever do those things again. I could feel the blood pounding in my temples. It kept time. It spoke, "You're dead. You're dead. Boom! Boom! You're dead."

I tried to find the Christian radio station from Minneapolis and St. Paul, but as I turned the radio dial, I heard station after station giving details of the storm and advising people to take cover. I had decided to go home on rural country roads and avoid the highway. I was in the middle of farm country. The farm houses were few and far between and I was certain there were no gas stations on these roads.

Despite my slow speed, the car kept hydroplaning. I realized I needed to pull over. As I slowed, looking for a place to park along the shoulderless road, I heard a crack of thunder so loud it shook the entire car and caused my ears to ring. My temples pounded harder and faster, "You're dead. You're dead. Boom! Boom! You're dead."

At that moment I realized how much I wanted to live and I wasn't ashamed to admit it. "Please, God! Help me through this storm!" The radio was all static now. I couldn't tune in any station. Another crack of thunder. My temples pounded faster and faster. *This is stupid,* I thought. *People have faced far greater challenges than this thunderstorm.* Nevertheless, I quoted the Twenty-third Psalm, "Even though I walk through the valley of the shadow of death, I will fear no evil."

Then, just as if I'd entered the storm through its front door, I suddenly exited out its back door. The storm was behind me—just like that! The sun was out and shining brightly. My temples pounded, "You're alive!" "You're alive! Boom! Boom! You're alive!"

I don't think the children understood why Daddy hugged them so hard when he got home. And that evening, as I sang "The Impossible Dream" in the *Man of La Mancha* play—despite the fever, despite the weak lungs—I had developed a new appreciation for the words of the song which encourage us, like Don Quixote, to continue on, no matter how difficult the journey.

I wish that everyone could stare death in the face before it's his or her time to die. Unfortunately, most of us aren't given an opportunity like Scrooge in Dickens's *The Christmas Carol* or like Jimmy Stewart in the classic movie *It's a Wonderful Life.* None of us will have an opportunity like Emily Webb Gibbs in Thornton Wilder's *Our Town.* It's so ironic, but only when we lose or are about to lose something do we realize how much we value it.

In all of this talk about growing older and dying, I don't want to forget the other end of life—the kids. Students in my classes always enjoy the *carpe diem* poems. "Seize the Day!" "Gather ye rosebuds while ye may..." Kids seem to have a clearer perception of how adults are so caught up in the rush, rush, and that we have little time for the hush, hush. Corny? Perhaps. But true.

◆

It's so ironic, but only when we lose or are about to lose something do we realize how much we value it.

◆

Kids are amazed at the things we consider matters of life and death. They ask us to play when we know we must work. Life is so serious to us, but they have not yet discovered how burdensome it is. Kids have a lot more time to laugh. And sing. And swing on swings.

I love working with kids. They help you strip through the pretense and catch a glimpse once again of childhood innocence. They remind you of simpler days, when life was not so cluttered, when you dreamed big dreams and had not yet decided that they could never come true. Next to a death sentence, this glimpse is about the best cure there is for someone grown cold or unappreciative of life.

Who can hold a baby in his arms and listen to its sounds and look into its eyes and smell the freshness of a new human being and not be flooded with a thousand different emotions? Oh, how far you've come from your days in the cradle. Oh, how close we are to the grave.

Jesus loves kids. Scripture reports:

> People were bringing little children to Jesus to have him touch them, but the disciples rebuked them. When Jesus saw this, he was indignant. He said to them, "Let the little children come to me, and do not hinder them, for the kingdom of God belongs to such as these. I tell you the truth, anyone who will not receive the kingdom of God like a little child will never enter it." And he took the children in his arms, put his hands on them and blessed them.
>
> (Mark 10:13-16)

Can't you picture it? Jesus with the children in his arms? I know that this passage speaks of the childlike faith which is necessary for salvation, but isn't it also saying that we have to be like little children in our approach to life? We must grow in maturity. We must accept responsibility. We must face the challenges and the burdens of life. But like little children we should have complete trust. Like little children we should awaken each day expecting a great adventure.

Occasionally I ask my students to write their own *carpe diem* poems. Sometimes we write them collectively as a class. Here's a sample:

Life passes quickly—
it doesn't go slow.
Today is gone
before you know!

Tomorrow is here—
and then it is past.
Then tomorrow is yesterday—
my, it goes fast!

Yesterday, yesterday—
where is today?
Oh, please slow down!
I just want to play!

But faster and faster—
like a runaway train.
Life's going so fast—
I'm going insane.

Did you hear me?
Did you hear what I said?
I'm going insane!
Never mind, I'm dead.

Oh, I know, Shakespeare said it so much better:

Tomorrow and tomorrow and tomorrow creep in this
petty pace from day to day and to the last syllable
of recorded time, and all our yesterdays have
lighted fools the way to dusty death. Out! Out!
brief candle. Life is but a walking shadow, a poor
player who struts and frets his hour upon the stage
and then is heard no more. 'Tis a tale told by an
idiot, full of sound and fury, signifying nothing.

Life is but a walking shadow—a candle that will soon be extinguished. The writer of the book of Job said the same thing, you know?

> Remember, O God, that my life is but a breath.
>
> (Job 7:7)

> Our days on earth are but a shadow.
>
> (Job 8:9)

> Man born of woman is of few days...He springs up
> like a flower and withers away; like a fleeting shadow,
> he does not endure.
>
> (Job 14:1-2)

I remember when I was a kid I read a little tract called "The Clock." It went something like this:

> *The clock of life is wound but once,*
> *And no man has the power*
> *To tell just when the hands will stop*
> *At late or early hour.*
>
> *To lose one's wealth is sad indeed.*
> *To lose one's health is more.*
> *To lose one's soul is such a loss*
> *That no man can restore.*

The tract declared that 39 people died during the time it took to read the poem and that more than 5,400 people die every hour. When I was in college I used to recite this poem and these statistics to kids to whom I witnessed. I was known as a "fanatic." But I would recite the poem, look my peers in the eye, and ask, "Are you ready to meet your Maker?"

The day I died I came home convinced that I wasn't really ready to meet my Maker. Oh, I knew that if I had died I had the assurance of eternal life, but I also had caught a glimpse of the fact that God had other things in mind for me in this life. I also realized that my priorities were way out of order and I had to learn how to do what the *carpe diem* poets suggested several centuries ago, "Gather ye rosebuds while ye may."

♦

*When you catch a glimpse
of death, it's amazing how so many things
you think vitally important aren't even in
the picture; and the things that you've been
taking for granted, the things that you can't
buy, those are suddenly the things
of matchless value.*

♦

Driving home from Collegeville that day with my temples pounding, "You're dead! You're dead!" I never once thought of speaking engagements I would have to cancel. I never thought of bills or worried about their payment. I never thought how much I'd like a bigger house or a nicer car. I thought about my family, of Tammy's warm embrace, and her wonderful sense of humor. Oh, how I'd miss those! And the kids...my kids...our kids...Could I ever hold them long enough? Spend enough time with them? Read enough books to them? Say enough prayers with them?

When you catch a glimpse of death, it's amazing how so many things you think vitally important aren't even in the picture; and the things that you've been taking for granted, the things that you can't buy, those are suddenly the things of matchless value.

I'm planning to be around for at least another forty years, but then again, I never know for sure and neither do you. Next summer, the good Lord willing, you know what I plan to do? I'm going to take my children, Seth, Luke, Jessica and Zachary to the Nisswa Turtle Races. Maybe I'll see you there. Oh, don't worry about not having your own turtle. You can rent them right there. Maybe your turtle will get lucky and win the grand prize. It's worth..........$5.00.

Profile of a Saint

Before he died they called him one of the three "pillars of the church." But it didn't begin that way.

It was a humble home. There was no television, VCR, or video games. No microwave oven. No gas or electric range. No running water. No electricity. They were a close family. His brothers and sisters had a childhood filled with lots of laughter, and as the boys grew they worked alongside their father in his shop and learned his trade. But none of them ever thought they'd see the day they could master the craft as well as their dad.

His oldest brother had been acting strange ever since that day the family went to the city and he got lost. The family had agonized while searching for him for three days. He had never seen his parents so worried. They had checked with all the other relatives, but He wasn't with them. They checked with the authorities, but no child had been found. His mom and dad found it difficult to believe that their oldest son had run away from home. After all, theirs was a happy family and a healthy home. His brother had expressed no displeasure and had shown no signs of rebellion or anger.

He remembered the look his father had given him when he asked, "Do you think he's been kidnapped?"

Finally, after searching throughout the city his parents found his brother sitting in the Temple School asking and answering questions as though He were a rabbi! When they found Him, his mother grabbed Him. He was unsure whether out of relief or out of anger, she begged Him, "Why did you do this to us? Your father and I have been sick with worry! We've looked everywhere for you!"

He couldn't believe Jesus' answer. Jesus looked at His parents who had been searching for Him for three days, and all He said was, "You didn't need to search for me. I had to be here at my Father's House. Don't you realize this?" James remembered the look his parents exchanged. It was a slow, deliberate look as they both stared deep into one another's eyes. Was there a smile in his mother's eyes? What did Jesus mean? Even though they seemed to know something James did not know, they made Jesus promise He'd never leave them like that again without first asking permission and telling them where He was going. James was amazed that they did not punish Him.

James had heard about the school where Jesus had been found. This being the Passover, rabbis from all over the land had gathered at the Temple School to discuss the great truths and promises of Scripture. An older man who had been at the school said to his father, "Joseph, your Son, Jesus, spoke with the wisdom of the coming Messiah. The rabbis believe that Messiah will come very soon!"

"Yes," said Joseph, "the Messiah is coming soon." James did not know then that his half-brother, Jesus, was God's Son, the

Messiah, the Savior, the Christ. His parents knew, but even they could not comprehend the full extent of their Son's ministry or His Mission. They tried to treat Him like they treated their other children, but nothing was ever quite the same again after that moment at the Temple School.

The family returned to Nazareth. The boys went back to work in the carpenter shop alongside their dad. But Jesus became increasingly wise, and when He talked of spiritual things, people listened. He spoke not as a carpenter, not even as a rabbi, He spoke with authority uncommon to men.

Years passed. One day as Jesus was talking to some people in the carpenter shop, James felt a tug on his arm. He turned and looked, and there stood his brothers Jude and Simon. Jude took hold of his arm. Together they walked a distance away from Jesus where their conversation could not be heard. "Who does He think He is, anyhow?" was Jude's question.

"I wonder, too," said James, "He talks continually of the Kingdom of Heaven. He talks like He's an authority. He's never been to seminary. He's a carpenter, just like the rest of us, just like Dad."

"It's embarrassing," said Simon. "Some of my friends tell me that they think our brother, Jesus, has gone way overboard with His constant talk about God."

"He's just 30 years old," said James, "and He doesn't seem to have any interest in taking a wife. He indicated to me the other day that He's going to be leaving home soon to begin a ministry of His own!"

"What?" asked Jude. "Who does He think He is?"

"Mother said He plans to seek out this Baptist fellow, John, who's been baptizing people in the Jordan River. I guess Jesus wants to be baptized and become His disciple." Simon found His brother's behavior impossible to accept.

"No," said James, "He may want John to baptize Him but I don't think He could ever be happy being a disciple. The way I've heard Him talk I think He wants people to follow *Him*."

"Who does He think He is?" asked Jude again.

"I hate to admit that He's my brother sometimes," added Simon.

A few days later Jesus walked out of the carpenter shop never to return again. Mary knew, then, that His time had come—yet she did not yet totally understand.

Every day someone brought a new report of what Jesus had supposedly done. James and his brothers and sisters could not believe it when they heard Jesus had healed a leper.

One report said, "Your brother was in Capernaum and He was preaching to a large crowd. There were so many people the house couldn't hold them all! Well, four men came carrying a man who was paralyzed. They wanted to see if your brother could heal him, but they couldn't get anywhere close to Him because the house was so full of people. So you know what they did? They took a section of the roof off the house and lowered the paralytic down with ropes on a stretcher. And your brother healed him! Sure enough! The guy threw down his bed and got up and walked. Everyone was amazed!"

James thought, *I bet the guy wasn't really paralyzed.* Another report came, "Your brother, Jesus healed someone on the Sabbath and was rebuked by the Pharisees. But your brother talked right back to them. I've never seen the Pharisees so angry. There's talk they want to have Him put away. You better warn Him."

James answered, "I can do nothing."

And again the report came, "Your brother, Jesus, ah, did you hear about the men that are following Him? I guess He hand-picked a group of twelve guys made up of fishermen, a tax collector, and I don't know what the others do, but I guess they all just left what they were doing and now travel with Him around the country. You know, James, some people say that He is insane...Others are saying He is the Messiah."

One day after more reports and more rumors, James went to Mary, his mother. "Mother," he said, "we must go to Jesus and see for ourselves what He is doing. We must warn Him that the Pharisees seek to harm Him. I will get Simon, Jude, and my brother, Joseph, and we must go. I wish Father were alive, maybe He could talk some sense into Him."

Mary and Jesus' brothers came to Him while He was teaching in a crowded house. As soon as they arrived and saw that it was impossible to get close to Jesus, they sent word to Him that they were in the audience and they would like to visit. But Jesus did not quit teaching, not even for a moment. James was infuriated when he heard that Jesus had made the comment that everyone in the audience was His brother and sister. How could He love these people as much as the family with whom He had spent His first 30 years?

Weeks passed. The family heard more reports.

"Your brother calmed the storm by simply rebuking the sea!"

"Your brother cast demons out of the man who lived in the graveyard. The man is telling everyone of your brother's great mercy!"

"Your brother brought a dead child back to life! Some say the little girl was only sleeping, but we know she was truly dead!"

And then, at last, His brother came home to Nazareth, His hometown. James was glad to see him, but when Sabbath came and Jesus stood and taught in the synagogue, the town was buzzing with gossip.

"He has no formal training!"

"He's just a carpenter!"

"He's Mary's boy, and His brothers and sisters live right here in town!"

"Who does He think He is! He's no better than anybody else!"

James couldn't help but hear the comments. Oh, there were those who were astounded by Jesus' wisdom, but most in Nazareth could not accept that someone they knew could possibly be the Messiah. James heard his brother explain to a crowd that He had come home hoping to work great miracles among them, but their unbelief prevented Him. There were reports of a few minor healings, but Jesus left town without raising any dead people, or healing any lepers.

Jesus' words rang in James' ears: "A prophet is not honored by his own people—not even by his own family."

The reports did not stop coming to Nazareth after Jesus had left there.

"King Herod had John the Baptist beheaded! He wants to kill Jesus, too!"

"Jesus fed five thousand people with but five loaves of bread and two fish!"

"Jesus walks on water!"

"Jesus gives sight to the blind!"

"Peter, the fisherman, one of his disciples, says that Jesus is the Messiah!"

James heard all the reports. Someone said that Jesus had indicated He would die soon. The man who had told him this, sensing James' pain, quickly added, "But He said that He would rise again after three days in the grave."

"Only God could do that," said James.

He didn't go to the crucifixion. Neither did his brothers and he begged his mother not to go, but she went nonetheless. He'd heard about crucifixions. He couldn't imagine a more horrible way to die. People would come from miles around to watch. It was like a carnival. His brother, Jesus, half naked, would be hanging there on a cross while the crowd taunted him with shouts of, "Save yourself if you are the Messiah! Save yourself!"

Had it been 20 years since they were boys together, wrestling on the floor? Where had the years gone? What had happened to Jesus? James had lost his brother, his friend. And now his mother. She believes all that Jesus said. She's gone to live in the house of one of his brother's followers, John. James asked himself, "Have I also lost my mother?"

Mary told him of the crucifixion, "In the midst of His suffering He spoke directly to His Father in heaven," she said. "He pleaded, 'Forgive them for they know not what they do!'"

James couldn't accept that story. How can you forgive someone who has nailed you to a tree and left you there to die? How can you forgive someone who spits in your face and opens your back with whips? Forgive them! Impossible!

Joseph of Arimathea took His body from the cross. "Ironic," thought James, *my father's name...my brother's name...Joseph."* His mother said that one of the members of the Sanhedrin, a man by the name of Nicodemus, provided embalming ointment of myrrh and aloes. "Myrrh," thought James. Hadn't he heard a rumor long ago that Jesus had received myrrh when he was born? His parents had never talked about it, but there were reports that Jesus had been visited by astronomers who had presented Him gifts.

Joseph and Nicodemus carried Jesus' body to a tomb not far from the site of the crucifixion and there they laid him. They sealed the opening of the tomb with a boulder. He'd never see his brother again.

James went to bed on Saturday night, but he couldn't sleep. Over and over in his mind he thought, *He said if He died He would rise and live again in three days.* He heard himself answer, "Only God can do that."

It didn't take long for the reports to reach him that Sunday. The stone had been rolled away. The tomb was empty. The body was missing. People speculated:

"He wasn't really dead!"

"I bet His disciples stole His body!"

"No, I think the Romans stole His body!"

"There are a few people who say they've seen Him."

"Impossible! I was there at the crucifixion and He was dead! He can't come back to life again!"

Days went by. More reports. More theories. "Why couldn't they just let Him die?" All of the talk and all of the speculation just made James feel worse.

One report indicated that Jesus had appeared to Simon Peter, whom they called Cephas. Another report claimed that Jesus appeared to over five hundred people at one time and all of them swore that it was truly Him.

"Oh, God!" cried James. "Just let my brother die!"

Dear reader, as you know, I've taken a great deal of literary license here. There are some Christians who accept the ancient tradition that Mary had no children other than Jesus. If this is the way you believe, you may feel this story is downright insulting. Most scholars today, however, believe that the Bible is very clear when it talks about the brothers and sisters of Jesus.

I believe that Jesus had siblings and I believe that James was his half-brother (Matt.12:46-50; 13:55; Mark 3:21, 31-35; John 7:3-9). If this is true, then everything in this story is within the realm of possibility. It's plausible. I've tried to present it in such a way that you can actually picture it happening, but now I'm stumped. Look what the Bible says about Jesus' resurrection appearances:

> Christ died for our sins according to the Scriptures, that he was buried, that he was raised on the third day according to the Scriptures, and that he appeared to Peter, and then to the Twelve. After that he appeared to more than five hundred of the brothers at the same time, most of whom are still living, though some have fallen asleep.
>
> (1 Cor. 15:3-6)

Now, get this!

> Then he appeared to James, then to...
> (1 Cor. 15:7)

How do you think He did it? How did He appear to him? Was James sleeping then awakened to find Christ standing at the end of his bed? Was he eating when suddenly Jesus joined him at the table?

Or did James hear a voice speaking to him, asking, "James, do you remember when we were kids and how you and Jude use to hide under the bed and ask Me to try to find you? I'd search for ten minutes even though I knew where you were. You used to laugh and jump up and down and say, 'We won! We won!' Do you remember that, James?"

I can imagine James hearing His voice then suddenly seeing Christ. I suspect He threw himself at His feet and called him "Lord".

The Bible is clear about a number of things. James wrote a letter to the Jewish Christian Church. He begins his letter with these words, "James, a servant of God and of the Lord Jesus Christ" (Jas. 1:1).

I would probably have started the letter like this, "James, half-brother of Jesus, sometime wrestling champion, and constant hide-and-seek victor, writing to you about my firsthand experiences with my brother who is the Lord and Savior of the world."

But not James. He never boasts. He never mentions his special relationship to Christ. Neither does Jude in his letter. Jude calls himself a servant, too. But Jude does mention that he is a brother of James.

What's my point? Simply this, saints are servants. From the moment the resurrected Jesus appeared to him, James became a totally committed servant of his Lord.

The Book of Acts opens with the story of Christ's ascension into heaven. He had spent 40 days after His resurrection instructing the disciples. His last words to them were:

> Do not leave Jerusalem, but wait for the gift my
> Father promised, which you have heard me speak
> about. For John baptized with water, but in a few days
> you will be baptized with the Holy Spirit.
> (Acts 1:4-5)

And then he said to them:

> You will receive power when the Holy Spirit comes
> on you; and you will be my witnesses in Jerusalem,
> and in all Judea and Samaria, and to the ends of the
> earth. (Acts 1:8)

And then he left them.

Now they wait for this power that was promised them. Holy Spirit power! Pentecostal power! In the Upper Room they wait, about 120 of them. Can you see the faces in the crowd? Waiting faces?

There's Thomas. He doubts no more.

There's Peter, whose false pride died that night outside the gate when he denied his Lord.

Matthias, traitorous Judas's replacement, waits.

All who really believe are right here.

Think about it. This small group, here in the Upper Room, holds the future of Christianity in their hands—your salvation and mine. It would be far easier for them all to go home, go back to their former jobs, their previous lives—go home and turn on their television sets and forget Christ's commandment to be His witnesses to the ends of the earth. Why, telling others about Jesus could be hazardous to their health! Why not just go home?

But they don't go home. They wait. They've seen. They believe. Now they can do nothing other than serve. There is no other choice. Christ has proven He is who He said He was. They've seen. And although there are only 120 here, they wait for the power. They know they can never do what has been commanded of them without the power.

On the day He ascended they had stood staring into the clouds long after He was gone. They had stood gazing intently until the angel spoke to them. "He's coming back," the angel said, "just as He ascended, he will descend again."

A few days pass and they are praying on their knees in the Upper Room now.

There's John, the beloved.

There is James, son of Alphaeus.

There is Matthew, the former tax collector.

There is Bartholomew and Andrew and Philip.

There is Jesus' mother, Mary.

There is James. See him? He's on his knees beside his mother, Mary, and he's in fervent prayer. (Historians record that in only a few short years James was given the nickname "The Just." His knees became hard and calloused like a camel's knees from so many hours kneeling in prayer.)

They all wait for the power of the Holy Spirit and they pray.

Finally the Spirit comes.

♦

Because of these saints and their commitment, you and I know about Christ today. Tradition holds that every one of the disciples except John died a martyr's death.

♦

It sounds like a tornado coming down from heaven. Tongues of fire dance and rest on each of them. The Holy Spirit fills them and they speak in languages they do not understand, although other Jews who witness the event understand them clearly. The believers declare the wonders of God and His Son Jesus Christ!

Peter preaches a sermon with great boldness. "Repent and be baptized, every one of you in the name of Jesus Christ so that your sins may be forgiven" (Acts 2:38).

That day many believers are added to their numbers. People are healed and miraculous signs and wonders are exhibited. Christianity is alive and growing!

Because of these saints and their commitment, you and I know about Christ today. Tradition holds that every one of the disciples except John died a martyr's death.

What about James?

James became one of "the pillars of the church" (Gal. 1:19). Most theologians agree that his letter is the most precise instruction manual found in the Bible. Only 108 verses in length and yet over 60 verses are commands for believers on ways to put faith into practice. Faith without works is dead (Jas. 2:17).

James became the head of the church in Jerusalem. He presided over the Council of Jerusalem which allowed Gentiles to enter the Christian Church (Acts 12:17).

Paul met with James when he first came to Jerusalem as a believer and later he brought to James the collection from the Gentile churches in Asia (Acts 21:18-25).

Saint James! See his camel's knees? What does he pray for on those knees?

Historians report that James was brought before the Jewish High Priests and members of the Sanhedrin. Ananias, the High Priest, was angry at the large numbers of Jews who were becoming Christians. According to Josephus, James was commanded to stand on one of the balconies of the Temple and proclaim to an assembled crowd that Jesus was not the Messiah.

Imagine it. A large crowd assembles. James stands on the ledge of the balcony with the guards and with Ananias. The High Priest commands everyone's silence. If James wants to live he knows what he has to say. He must denounce Jesus Christ.

All eyes are on him as James boldly shouts, "Jesus is the Son of God, the Savior and Judge of the world!"

Immediately the guards are on him. They throw him from the balcony. An angry crowd mocks and kicks him. They throw stones at him, still James rises to those knees—those camel knees. As they beat him to death with clubs, he looks toward heaven and prays, "Father, forgive them, for they know not what they do."

At the moment of James' death, Ananias rejoices, for he has seen James killed.

At the moment of his death, James, too, rejoices. For in that moment, he sees Jesus.

Precious in the sight of the Lord is the death of his saints!
(Ps.116:15)

There's a Light in the Window

I love the radio commercial for a motel chain that promises they'll leave a light on for me. It gives me a warm feeling knowing that somewhere a light is on and someone is waiting up for me.

I imagine that God has a light on in the window of heaven, too, and He is waiting for all of His children to come home.

But we wander—some of us wander so far we never come back. I've been a wanderer, a wayward saint, but I've seen the light and I'm on my way home.

As a kid I used to listen to Dion and the Belmonts. I'd sing along with Dion as he sang

> *I'm the kind of guy*
> *who likes to roam around.*
> *I'm never in one place,*
> *I roam from town to town.*
> *And when I find myself*

falling for some girl,
I hop into my car and I
roam around the world.

I'm a wanderer, a wanderer,
I roam from town, to town, to town....

How's that for commitment! We laugh at Dion's song but when it comes to our Christian commitment, it's not a laughing matter.

During the war in the Persian Gulf, yellow ribbons began appearing on trees and on car antennas. One airline company even had yellow ribbons painted on its planes.

"What are all the yellow ribbons for, Dad?" asked our son, Seth.

"They are a symbol," I said. "They stand for the fact that we want all of our soldiers to come home safely."

Of course, our children are too young to remember the song about yellow ribbons that was popular during the Vietnam war, so I sang them a few bars:

Tie a yellow ribbon 'round the old oak tree,
It's been three long years, do you still love me?

I was dismayed to discover that I had forgotten the rest of the words to the song. The only other part I remembered was the end. Remember? The guy comes home and he finds a hundred yellow ribbons tied around the old oak tree.

I always loved that song. How could I have forgotten the words? When was the last time I sang them?

It's 1973. Billy Graham is preaching at the State Fairgrounds near St. Paul, Minnesota. I had accepted Christ after watching the Billy Graham movie *The Restless Ones*. Billy Graham was one of my heroes. Now here I was on my way to see Dr. Graham in person! And to have the opportunity to hear George Beverly Shea sing! And to watch Cliff Barrows direct the choir! It was too good to believe.

Bruce was driving, John was in the passenger's seat, and I was in the back. All three of us loved to sing, so from Brainerd to St. Paul we sang, each trying to outsing the other. IT WAS LOUD! Sometimes we were off-key. (Not me, of course!) We tried to harmonize. We sang hymns and popular songs. John didn't know many of the good old hymns because he'd grown up in a church where they hadn't sung them. "What a shame," I thought.

I'll never forget that moment. We were singing "Tie a Yellow Ribbon," which was then at the top of the pop charts, when all of a sudden we saw an oak tree covered with a hundred yellow ribbons the entire length of its trunk. It was one of those moments you just don't forget.

John and Bruce were two of my best college friends and it was a privilege to share this special moment with them. I figured our days together were numbered. I had such noble intentions of staying in touch with my high school friends, but it hadn't worked out that way, and I figured that it wouldn't be much different with my college friends.

But I was wrong. Bruce and I are still friends to this day, although we rarely see each other. And, John? Well, he'll always hold a very special place in my heart. John became a wanderer.

After graduating from college, I didn't see John for over a year. When I finally made contact with him, I thought he sounded different. We agreed to meet for coffee at a restaurant. I was looking forward to seeing one of my best friends again. I couldn't believe that a whole year had passed without any communication.

We met at Perkins Cake and Steak, one of only two restaurants in town that stayed open 24 hours a day. It was appropriate that we met at Perkins. John and I had spent many nights there, talking and boldly sharing our faith with whomever would listen. We used to go to the restaurant during "bar rush," that time when restaurants fill up with those who've closed down the bars and are often too wound up to go home. Often we'd see friends come in. We'd go sit with them, looking for opportunities to talk with them about the Lord.

Sometimes we'd sit with complete strangers, and at the slightest pause in the conversation we would pull out one of Campus Crusade for Christ's little booklets and ask, "Have you ever heard of the 'Four Spiritual Laws?'"

The fourth spiritual law says, "We must individually receive Jesus Christ as Savior and Lord; then we can know and experience God's love and plan for our lives." When we got to that law, John or I would ask, "Would you like to receive Jesus as your Savior? If the answer was yes, we'd take the person out to the car where we could pray the sinner's prayer with him.

I don't know how many times we went to the car, but I think the manager of Perkins must have wondered what was going on. Sometimes we'd take three or four people a night out to the parking lot and later we'd come back inside and sit down with someone else. Tim Gehris at Bethany Bible Bookstore kept us supplied with Four Spiritual law booklets, and the Holy Spirit kept prompting us to try to win just one more soul.

I look back at those times now and smile. They remind me of the story I heard of a semi–truck driver who loved to pick up hitchhikers in his big sixteen–wheeler. One day he picked up a man, who, almost before he was seated, noticed hundreds of notches in the truck's steering wheel and asked, "What are those notches for?" The semi–driver, removing a bowie knife from the sheath fastened to his belt, smiled and said, "Each notch is for one hitchhiker who came to know Jesus in this cab." And then, taking the knife, he made another notch, smiled at the hitchhiker and said, "You're number 227!"

Those were good days! Wonderful memories! And as I sat recalling all the good times, I was determined that the cherished friendship with John wasn't going to end like most of my high school friendships had.

I arrived at Perkins before John and asked for a booth in the "No Smoking" section. The hostess seated me in the same booth where John and I had sat many times. I kept my eyes glued to the entrance. I was anxious to see my friend and brother in Christ.

I hardly recognized him when he finally came. He looked as though he had aged ten tears in one. He seemed happy to see me, but apprehensive. "We've got so much catching up to do," I said as we sat down after our greeting, and then I quickly asked, "Have you ever heard of the Four Spiritual Laws?"

John smiled. We engaged in a bunch of small talk, did some reminiscing, and then he got very serious. "Guy, there is so mething I have to tell you."

"Okay," I said.

"I'm gay."

I don't think I answered him.

"I'm involved in a relationship," he said, and then told me about his housemate.

I didn't say a word. I couldn't.

Finally, John looked at me and asked, "Do you still want to be my friend?"

I answered too quickly, "Of course I'm your friend." Inside I felt sick. I was angry. I was confused. I made an attempt at talking about Jesus and the fact that homosexuality is an abomination in the eyes of God, but John's response to me was "I'm not so sure about God anymore." Instead of reminding John of the forgiveness that comes with repentance, I condemned him, and by the time we left the restaurant, I'm sure he felt I had decided there was no hope for him and had assigned him a proper place in hell. And, truly, that is what I had done.

Months passed. John and I had no further contact. I heard that he was working not far from where I lived, but I made no attempt to reach out to him.

Then, one week, I was working on a sermon based on Luke 15:11–31—the story of the prodigal son. One commentator noted that the story would be better called "the story of the loving father." Although I had heard the story many times, I found it difficult to believe that the father of the prodigal had such complete forgiveness for his son. The kid had wasted his entire inheritance! He had spent his money on prostitutes and alcohol! I found myself emphathizing with the elder son who had stayed home and been so faithful. "He's the one for whom the fatted calf should have been slaughtered!" I thought.

Picture it. The father stands in the doorway, waiting. He knows his son has been a fornicator. He knows his son has been a gambler. He knows his son has boozed it up, but he stands waiting, arms outstretched, ready to forgive and forget if his son will just come to his senses and *come home*. Perhaps if we listen we can even hear him softly singing, "Come home! Come home!"

That's grace! That's amazing grace! I can see the light in the window—and a million yellow ribbons tied to the gates of heaven for that prodigal boy.

As I worked on that sermon, I realized I had to tell John about the ribbons on heaven's gates—about the light in the window. I had to remind John that no matter what he had done there was forgiveness if he, like the prodigal son, would repent and come home. Sins forsaken are sins forgotten, and the loving Father waits with the fatted calf. God said clearly to me, "Remind John that there is always a light in the window."

As I thought about John and the conversation I wanted to have with him, God convicted me. He showed me area after area of my own life that I had not yet surrendered to Him. I realized it was only because of the Father's grace and mercy that I could know salvation.

I was driven. I had to talk to John before Sunday. I had to ask for his forgiveness for my cold heart, and I had to remind him of the yellow ribbons and the light in the window. I called him and asked if he could come to my home and talk. At first he sounded hesitant, but then he said he would and we set a time.

John left work a few days later and headed toward my house. I waited, but he didn't arrive. I called his workplace, but no one answered the phone. After another half hour and no sign of John and no answer to my calls, I decided to drive to the store where he worked and find out where he had gone.

I was a mile away, when I heard the sirens and saw the flashing lights. Nearing the accident, I saw his car. "Oh, God!" I screamed.

His body had already been removed and taken to the hospital. The tow truck was hoisting his car and hauling it to the junk yard. The car that had sideswiped John's was filled with drunken people, none of whom had been severely injured, but their drunken driving had killed my friend.

I didn't go to his funeral and I will forever regret it. I was a very immature 23–year–old kid. I had enrolled in a week–long graduate course. To attend the funeral would have meant losing my credit and the money I had paid for the course. Well, that was my excuse. The truth is, I was confused and completely torn apart inside.

Years passed. I repressed the memory of John and all my feelings of confusion and uncertainty about him. They lay buried beneath the soil of denial and fear. Recently, however, as I conducted my inventory of the past, I grieved John's death the way I should have fifteen year ago.

God never quit loving John. The light was always on, but I'll never know in this life if John came home.

Not too long ago I visited John's grave. I stood there a long time, remembering—crying. "John," I said, quite aware that he couldn't hear me, "I'm sorry. I love you. I just want everyone to know that there is a light on in the window and Jesus has tied a million ribbons around Heaven's gates."

And then I walked back to my car. But before I did, I bent over and placed a yellow ribbon next to where the stone read, "John."

Come Before Winter

everend Chester Olson faithfully served my boyhood church as pastor for over 25 years. How many sermons did he preach during that time? At least a thousand, I figure. Think of it. A thousand Sunday sermons, and that doesn't count funerals, weddings, and mid-week services.

I can still hear Reverend Olson's words at my grandparents' funerals, and his funeral words for my mom and my dad and Maude Dahl and Seed and Mamie Hand and Howard and Carrie and Signe and Fern...I know these are just names to you, but they were family to me.

How many funerals in 25 years?

When I first heard Reverend Olson speak, I have to admit I poked fun at him. His Scandinavian accent was about the heaviest I had ever heard. I can still remember him saying, "In your labor and in your rest." "Labor" ended up sounding liked "labe oar." But over the years, I developed an appreciation for Reverend Olson's accent and realized that it was one last vestige of the thousands of immigrants who had come to America and had labored to make our country the greatest nation in the world.

Every funeral I ever heard Reverend Olson conduct he always read these words:

> Let not your hearts be troubled; believe in God, believe also in Me. In My Father's house are many dwelling places. If this were not so, I would have told you. For I am going away to prepare a place for you. And when I have gone and prepared a place for you, I will come again and take you to Myself so that where I am, you also will be. And where I am going, you know the way.
>
> (John 14:1-4; RBV)

But when Reverend Olson read this Scripture he didn't use a translation that read, "In my Father's house are many dwelling places." No, I remember clearly, he read, "In my Father's house are many mansions."

A mansion! That's far better than "a dwelling place," don't you think?

When I was a kid I tried to use Mel Bay's methods to learn how to play the ukulele. One of the songs I could play fairly well was this one and of course, I'd sing along:

> *I've got a mansion, just over the hill top,*
> *in that bright land where I'll never grow old.*
>
> *And someday yonder, I will nevermore wander,*
> *but walk the streets that are purest gold!*

I didn't fully appreciate that song then. Read its words one more time. A mansion. You'll never grow old! You'll nevermore wander! The streets are pure gold!

Knowing that this is the destination awaiting God's saints is what allows us to accept the fullness of Christ's love in this life. But doesn't it break your heart when you see all the people who have never gotten even a glimpse of their heavenly mansion? Who's going to tell them about it? And when? What are we waiting for?

Of all the hundreds of sermons I ever heard Reverend Olson preach, I have one all-time favorite: "Come Before Winter." Maybe it's because I've always been a sucker for endings. I like to sit through movies until all the credits are finished. I like to watch sporting events until the teams have gone back into their locker rooms. I always lose it at graduation services, especially if a choir sings, "The Halls of Ivy" at the end. And I always read the last chapter of a book several times because—well, there is just something mighty important about endings.

I like beginnings, too. It's usually in the middle where things get a little bogged down. Life is like a good movie. You don't want to miss the beginning, and you just can't miss the ending, but in the middle you sometimes leave your seat and go out to the lobby to get some popcorn. When you come back you ask your partner, "What'd I miss?"

There's a movie of life called "Eternity with Christ." The sad thing is that most of the people in the theater are out in the lobby.

Sometimes a movie gets off to a slow start, just like life and you wonder if it'll ever get better. A good movie maker promises you a movie with a climactic ending that will send you from the theater revived and energized. Those are the kind of endings I like. That's the kind of ending Reverend Olson talked about in his

"Come Before Winter" sermon that I'll never forget. That's what God wants to do in our lives.

Paul sat in prison, a condemned man. The dungeon was cold and damp and lonely. Thirty years he had served his Lord. How many missionary journeys? How many converts? How many letters? How many beatings and imprisonments had he endured?

He had been a persecutor of Christians in his early life. But the many scars on his face and body were testimonies that the persecutor had become the persecuted, the villain had become the victim, the vilest offender had become the most righteous of saints.

Now there was just one more letter to write. He asks the guard for a pen and paper and tries to adjust his shackles. He knows that this will be his final letter.

To Timothy, my dearest son.

I remember how you cried when they arrested me and brought me here to Rome. I cried, too. I long to see you again, Timothy. I pray for you each day and thank God for you. I know how much you love and trust Him. Keep trusting Him, Timothy, and always be bold in Christ!

Paul continues to write. This letter becomes the most personal of all his other letters and conveys a great sense of urgency.

The Lord gives us strength in suffering, Timothy. I am in jail for serving Him, but never hesitate to serve Him for fear of suffering, because Jesus has destroyed death!

Timothy, I know in whom I believe and I know what He is going to do. I'm committed to Him. I have no doubts whatsoever that He will honor my commitment.

Sometimes it may seem like we have exhausted our energy and our faith is in short supply, but it is when we are weakest that He is strongest. He never lets us down. He always keeps His promises.

These are the words of a man in a dungeon waiting to be beheaded. When Reverend Olson preached that "Come Before Winter" sermon 25 years ago, I remember realizing for the first time that Paul was a human being—just like me. He was freezing in the dungeon. He was lonely. His heart ached for all those who rejected Christ. One last letter to write, and he writes it to Timothy.

During a time of personal devotions, I took that letter, now called *2 Timothy*, and I wrote it in my own words. What you have been reading above and what follows below is but a part of my paraphrase.

Dear, dear Timothy, my son! You have heard me preach many times of our Lord's plan of salvation. You must continue to tell the world, Timothy. You must never quit telling them, Timothy. You must be strong and help train others to go out and tell others who will go and tell others who'll continue to pass it on!

This will require much discipline, Timothy, and it will become harder and harder to be a Christian. People will have a head faith but not a heart faith.

They will love money more than they will love God.
The pursuit of pleasure will be their god. They will
think themselves wise but they are far from the truth.

But, Timothy, you've known the truth ever since
you were a child. You've studied the Scriptures all of
your life. Real wisdom leads to salvation through faith
in our Lord, Jesus, the Christ.

Now stop here for a minute. We've tried to picture Paul writing this letter, but what about Timothy? How do you think he felt knowing that he'd received the last words Paul ever penned? Here were instructions from a man about to die.

♦

*If you were to sit down and
write a last letter to your spouse or your
significant other or to your children, what
would you write? Why not write
those letters now?*

♦

If you were to sit down and write a last letter to your spouse
or your significant other or to your children, what would you
write? Why not write those letters now?

Paul brings his letter to a close:

Keep preaching, Timothy! People won't like it, but
keep preaching anyhow. People will look for preachers

who will tell them what they want to hear. They will look for preachers who could care less about the authority of God's Word—preachers who disregard Scripture and invent their own standards that allow them to live anyway they choose. These people will believe in fairy tales before they will believe in the Bible. But don't give up, Timothy! Keep preaching!

And now, nearing the end, this grand, old warrior who once wanted to see every follower of Christ put to death becomes even more personal. His heart hangs on every word.

I am going to be executed, Timothy. The time has come for me to depart this world. I pray that you can come and visit me soon.

I'm not worried about dying. Ever since I became His follower I have faced challenge after challenge, but Jesus has always given me the victory! I kept the faith, Timothy, and now the road of my life has come to an end. I look down it and do you know what I see? Jesus! And he waits to put a crown upon my head!

Then Paul's foretaste of glory divine is suddenly tempered with the reality of his present situation.

Please come quickly, Timothy.
Everyone except Luke has deserted me. The others did not have a faith that could stand the test. They preferred the things of this world. They will get their reward.

When you come, please bring Mark with you. And will you please bring my coat? Bring my books, too. And don't forget to bring my Bible.

That last line blows me away. Only days before his death and he asks for the "parchments." The Scriptures. Still studying the Scriptures, never finishing his meditation on God's Word.

Only a couple of lines of the letter are left now:

You must come soon, Timothy. Travel will be almost impossible unless you come before winter. Come before winter or it will be too late.

I'm praying that the Holy Spirit will always fill your life with all that Jesus is.

In His Grip,

Paul, Christ's Servant.

Of course, Reverend Olson finished his sermon by challenging us all to "come before winter."
Come before travel is impossible.
Come while the sun is still shining.
Come while you still can.
Come!

We don't know if Timothy made it in time or not. We don't know if he arrived before winter. It's not important, but what is important is whether or not you and I will make it. Are we really living the abundant life in Jesus Christ?

Like Paul, when our time comes to leave this world, will we be able to look at our lives and shout, "I have fought the good fight, I have finished the race, I have kept the faith!" (2 Tim. 4:7)?

How do you think Paul faced death the day they led him to the chopping block? I'm certain it was with complete assurance that at the moment his head was cut from his shoulders Jesus would be giving him a heavenly crown!

Now that's an ending!

Or is it the beginning?

If you are weary in the journey, come home before winter. Come to Christ. He's the only One with all the answers. This wayward saint is wayward no more. Now I see the way. Join me, and let's bring along all those who are living lives of quiet desperation. There is abundant life. Look down the road with me. Can you see Jesus waiting with your crown?

There is *Joy in the Journey* for those who believe.

ENDNOTES

Chapter 12

1 Research "Effects of Gender-Role Differentiation on U. S. High School Seniors, 1986, Johnston and O'Malley. Monitoring the Future: 1986, Institute for Social Research, University of Michigan and Cooperative Institutional Research Program, Higher Educational Research Group, Graduate School of Education, University of California, Los Angeles.

Chapter 13

1 Little, Paul E., *Know What You Believe*, (Wheaton, IL: Victor Books, 1970), p 25.

2 Swindoll, Charles R. *Growing Deep in the Christian Life*, Portland, OR: Multnomah Press, 1986, p. 93.

Chapter 15

1 "Christianity Today", William Iverson, *Christianity Today*, Carol Stream, IL: June 6, 1980, p. 33.

2 Ortiz, Juan Carlos, *Disciple*, (Lake Mary, FL: Creation House, 1975), p. 15.

3 Willard, Dallas, *The Spirit of the Disciplines:; Understanding How God Changes Lives*, (New York: Harper/Collins, Inc., 1988), p. 15-18.

4 Ibid.

Chapter 16

1 Halley, Henry, *Halley's Bible Handbook*, 24th Edition, (Grand Rapids, MI: Zondervan, 1965), p 245.